READING
WELLNESS

READING WELLNESS

Lessons in Independence
and Proficiency

JAN MILLER BURKINS & KIM YARIS
Foreword by Christopher Lehman

Stenhouse
PUBLISHERS

Portland, Maine

Stenhouse Publishers
www.stenhouse.com

Credits
Page 103: "A Storm Is Coming" by Keith Pigdon, series Explorations®, published exclusively in the USA by Okapi Educational Publishing Inc. www.myokapi.com, © EC Licensing Pty Ltd 2003–2014. Page 181: Graphic organizer for Heart, Head, Hands, and Feet lessons, copyright © 2013 Literacyhead.com.

Library of Congress Cataloging-in-Publication Data

Burkins, Jan Miller, 1968-
  Reading wellness : lessons in independence and proficiency / Jan Burkins, Kim Yaris.
    pages cm
  ISBN 978-1-62531-015-6 (paperback) -- ISBN 978-1-62531-020-0 (ebook) 1. Reading. 2. Reading comprehension. 3. Reading--Aids and devices. I. Yaris, Kim. II. Title.
  LB1050.42.B87 2014
  372.47--dc23

                                                              2014010230

Cover design, interior design, and typesetting by Alessandra S. Turati

Manufactured in the United States of America

PRINTED ON 30% PCW
RECYCLED PAPER

20 19 18 17 16 15 14   9 8 7 6 5 4 3 2 1

For Kim,
because "it is not often someone comes along who is a
true friend and a good writer."—E. B. White
J. B.

For Craig,
who brings joy and passion to all
aspects of my life.
K. Y.

CONTENTS

 # FOREWORD

As a child, I remember visits to Dr. Wood's office. He was our family doctor, a title that quite literally fit: his regular patients included my immediate family, my grandmother and grandfather, and a slew of aunts, uncles, and cousins. He was friendly, caring, and—as a small, squirmy child, I recall—talkative. It felt as if 10 percent of a checkup or sick visit was spent with him actually checking up, and the other 90 percent talking about family, friends, and life with one of my parents.

Aside from the occasional needle, his office felt like an extension of our home. "How's your grandma doing?" he would ask me, though of course he knew; he had just spent time talking with her the week before. What I began to learn was that caring was so much more than taking a temperature and administering antibiotics. It was about really listening, about developing whole lives.

Medical practice has shifted quite a lot since then. As accountability and insurance paperwork systems have grown more burdensome, and costs and patient loads have risen, many physicians describe feeling disillusioned with the profession they at one time felt called to enter.

In her book *What Doctors Feel: How Emotions Affect the Practice of Medicine* (Beacon Press, 2013) on the impact of emotions on medical care, Dr. Danielle Ofri describes a study of hospital-based doctors. These "hospitalists" were found to spend an average of just 17 percent of their day in direct patient care: "The vast majority of their time is spent documenting, reviewing medical records, communicating with other staff members, and handling paperwork." Primary care doctors, like my Dr. Wood, today fall into a similar, increasingly paper-heavy, patient-light reality. The further practitioners get from their patients, the less they feel connected to their profession.

It is not the case that physicians want to spend less time with patients. Just as it is not that we, in our own caring profession, signed up to administer yearly high-stakes tests, or shuffle our students from one benchmarking cycle to the next.

As districts across the country grapple with the Common Core State Standards, testing, and a slew of other Race to the Top initiatives, more and more classrooms are being pressured into adopting initiatives, "shifts," and programs that consider data more important than people and "complex texts" more critical than readers.

Even in schools that have refused to put programs above best practices—and thank goodness there are many—there remains a palpable fear: "Are we moving our students fast enough? Our levels high enough? Is there enough complexity?" As Donalyn Miller writes in *Reading in the Wild: The Book Whisperer's Keys to Cultivating Lifelong Reading Habits* (Jossey-Bass, 2013), *"Our zealous national focus on standardized test performance, often at the expense of meaningful reading instruction and support, has caused us to lose sight of our true obligations regarding children's literacy—fostering their capacity to lead literate lives."*

Our challenge today, it seems, is akin to that of physicians: to do no harm.

Children are born primed to make the very best of themselves. They are naturally curious, thoughtful, energetic, and demanding of attention, learning, and love. Their brains are ready to learn. Just as knee scrapes seem to heal in seconds, so too do their understandings of the world develop at an astonishing rate. Children can go from seeing scribbles on the page to reading words or from tangential ramblings to having deep conversations about books, often during the course of just one school year. Their minds and bodies are wired with a natural drive to thrive.

Our best work happens when we align our instructional decisions to their strengths and next steps—when our children become our curriculum, their actions our data, their potential our standards.

What I love about *Reading Wellness* is that Jan and Kim invite us to consider our current reading instruction and ask if we are truly aligned with our children. It is all too easy to get wrapped up in "Text-Dependent Questions" lessons or "Complete Your Reading Log" goals. Here, instead, they suggest that we look more closely at the ways books help our children to build their

lives. They invite us to teach children to be the drivers of their reading lives—
to set goals, tackle struggles, and celebrate successes themselves. Their focus
on teaching not books themselves, but individual readers, is refreshing and a
welcome counterbalance to the frantic pace and bewildering tasks so many of us
find ourselves facing.

In this way, *Reading Wellness* is also a book about caring for ourselves.
When, for example, Jan and Kim write of teaching students to stop to breathe—
both literally and metaphorically—I find myself doing the same. When they
teach a lesson on not just assigning books to students but helping them seek out
their own reading plan as a "vehicle along the path to dreams," I can't help but
step back and reflect on my own reasons for teaching reading.

Reading Wellness is not a book about teaching core standards; it is about
teaching the core of our children—and, in turn, the core of ourselves. The
classrooms Jan and Kim describe are the classrooms I want for my own
children, for everyone's children. Places where learning to read books is as
important as learning to read oneself, and where those goals are fundamentally
linked. Places where educators feel empowered to create alignment between
their reasons for becoming a teacher and the exciting challenge of developing a
new generation of empowered, insightful youth.

In 1925, Dr. Francis W. Peabody closed a lecture to Harvard medical
students with this: "The secret of the care of the patient is in caring for the
patient." *Reading Wellness* reminds us that nothing is more essential to our
classrooms than caring for our children's minds, beliefs, and passions. It is a
prescription for student-centered instruction in the truest sense.

—CHRISTOPHER LEHMAN
March 2014

ACKNOWLEDGMENTS

Without the faith, hope, and love—not to mention hard work—of many, this book would not be. Writing acknowledgments is always humbling—for books with two authors, this is doubly so.

First, we would like to thank the many teachers and administrators who have allowed us to share our thinking and have invited us into their schools and classrooms to teach the lessons in *Reading Wellness*. Thank you to Vita Beyer, Matthew Bryant, Kate Buonomo, Lynn Burke, Amy Chiarello, Marguerite Cordova, Pam Fine, Lisa Friend, Jessica Gates, Melissa Graham, Jacqui Musto, Melissa O'Brien, and Xernona Thomas. We deeply appreciate the opportunity and space to test, revise, and refine our thinking. Working with you and your students has brought us joy.

We also send our warmest and sincerest thanks to the visionary people at Stenhouse, who immediately "got" the ideas within *Reading Wellness*. In particular, we send unending thanks—and enormous bear hugs—to Dan Tobin and Philippa Stratton, who work to support teachers, students, and writers as whole people. The wise and kind Maureen Barbieri supported us lovingly throughout the publication process. Her feedback was *always* exactly what we needed to hear, and, without fail, her insight and guidance made *Reading Wellness* better. Thank you for pushing us, Maureen, while also helping us stay true to ourselves.

We each owe a debt of gratitude to people we would like to acknowledge individually, in the "I" person. These individuals have loved us, guided us, and supported us.

From Kim

First and foremost, I need to say thank you to Twitter, for without it, I would never have met Jan. Though it sounds a bit hokey, that chance meeting on the Internet now feels a lot like kismet. Meeting Jan was like finding a professional soul mate, and that alone would have been enough. However, in the process of writing a daily blog and book, I have also found a friend and confidante who, throughout the writing of this book, boosted my confidence and resolve. Thank you, Jan, for all that you bring to my life and, most of all, for helping me finally make it to "next week."

In addition to Jan, there have been many other colleagues who have influenced and shaped my thinking. Thank you to my study group: Patti Austin, Danielle Vedder, Leah Weissinger, Wanda Haggerty, Whitney O'Donnell, Anne Morris, Cara Newman, and Ferne Chase. I am so grateful for all of those Tuesday night conversations that helped me reflect on my teaching and learning.

Also, I owe a great debt of gratitude to Ellen Best-Laimit, my mentor, friend, and former principal who not only believed in my ability to teach children but believed (and convinced me) that I had something to share with teachers as well. Through the years, she has repeatedly asked, "Are you writing this stuff down?" No one person has had a greater influence on my career than Ellen, and for that I am so appreciative.

I also need to thank my family. My mom and dad always told me they thought I might grow up to become a writer. I told them that I was going to become a teacher, but I think they might have known I could be both. I am so grateful not only that they believed in me, but also that they instilled the work ethic required to finish a book!

I am also thankful to my mother-in-law and father-in-law, Deena and Harvey, who have been a great source of moral support throughout the writing of this book. Also, my two sons, Matthew and Nathan, have contributed more than they will ever know. In addition to serving as my test subjects and long-term case studies in reading development, they have been extremely tolerant of the time my writing has taken away from being with them. Instead of complaining about my absence, they'd visit me in my basement writing retreat and ask, "How's the book going, mom?" Their youthful perspectives and joie de vivre constantly help me redefine what it means to be "well."

And finally, I thank my husband, Craig. He has served as my pillar of strength throughout the writing of this book. Whenever my resolve faltered, he encouraged. Whenever I slacked off, he coaxed. Whenever Jan and I figured something out, he cheered. His support has been unfailing, and without him this book could not have happened.

From Jan

If you are lucky enough, perhaps even blessed, to have a friend who helps you rise to your best self; who sees your seamy underbelly and doesn't flinch; and who says, in your staunchest moments of self-loathing, "Don't you get it? I love you," then you are truly lucky. I am one such fortunate soul, and in the presence of such profound friendship, writing a book is of little consequence. Kim Yaris, you are my kin.

Thank you, as well, to dear friends Holly Johnson and Peggy Terrell, my mindfulness mentor and my teaching mentor, respectfully. They both nudge and nurse me toward balance and wellness. Thanks also to my dear friend Craig Yaris, who is a wonderful combination of kind and smart, and to Barbara Sorensen, who always makes me think. And I can't resist offering an all-by-myself "thank you" to Dan Tobin. Dan, you have supported my work in so many ways over the last couple of years. Thank you for your kindness, confidence, and patience.

Of course, I want to thank my family. My father, Sam Brewer, has encouraged me throughout this writing process, offering unwavering support, as he has throughout my life. My mother, Sarah Brewer, has forever been a steadfast advocate for my creativity, and my stepmother, Cindy Brewer, was the first to suggest that writing might be my calling. Love and thanks to my four sons—Christopher, Duncan, Natie, and Victor—who provide relentless and essential distraction, not to mention fodder for writing. Finally, I am, as always, grateful to my husband, Nate, who is unflinching in his support of my efforts to grow personally and professionally. Nathaniel Burkins, you are my home.

Introduction

HOW WELL
ARE YOU?

---

*Tell me, what is it you plan to do with your one
wild and precious life?*

—MARY OLIVER

G o into an elementary school and talk to teachers. Listen to students read. You will probably notice an unsettling trend among readers and the teachers who love and work with them. Too many students have trouble answering questions such as "What do you love about reading?" "Who are your favorite authors?" "What are your favorite genres? Why?" "How is what you are reading changing the way you think?" "What books bring you such enjoyment that you forget you are reading?" And these days, too many teachers struggle to answer questions such as "What do you love about teaching?" "What daily teaching practices bring you such joy that you get lost in them?" and "How does your work with students help you discover your best self?"

So much of what trends in education focuses on fixing something in readers. Students not comprehending? Teach them these strategies. Students having difficulty figuring out words? Administer DIBELS and teach them phonics. Fluency issues? Timed readings are in order.

In his TEDx talk "The Happy Secret to Better Work," psychologist Shawn Achor (2011) says that "the absence of disease is not health," which makes us question our current models for reading instruction. Does the absence of traditionally defined reading difficulties equal "reading wellness"?

1

We can't help but wonder if vaccinating against "comprehenza," treating "decoderitis," or intervening to remedy a case of "robotitis" has led to inaccurate assumptions that all is well with our readers. Perhaps it is time to stop and ask students (and ourselves), "How are you?" Many people are likely to respond to this question with a cursory "I am well." Perhaps the better question, however, is "How well are you?" with the parallel question related to reading—"How well are the readers with whom you work?"

In routine exchanges, people often indicate "wellness" without really thinking about what it means; it means a lot, however. Coined in the 1950s the term *wellness* was described as "maximizing the potential of which the individual is capable" and maintaining "balance and purposeful direction" (Dunn 1961, 4). In *The 22 Non-Negotiable Laws of Wellness,* Greg Anderson adds that "Wellness is the complete integration of body, mind, and spirit—and the realization that everything we do, think, believe, and feel has an effect on our state of well-being" (1995, 3). Ultimately, wellness is about the ways in which we weave together all the facets of our lives to be our best selves.

So, what about those readers in your life? How will you intentionally help them find balance and purposeful direction in their reading lives? Are they maximizing their potential? Are they weaving together all the facets of their reading lives—reading for relaxation, reading for information, reading for meaning, reading fluently, selecting texts, and on and on—to become their best reading selves?

When we set the aforementioned definitions of wellness alongside our reading instruction, we realize that reading wellness extends beyond skills and strategies. Although we endorse teaching comprehension strategies, explicitly showing students how the written code works, and practicing fluency intentionally, the ultimate purpose of fluency work is not improved fluency; it is becoming a lifelong reader. Reading wellness includes all aspects of readership, from discovering favorite books and authors to working on fluency, from reading magazines to reading directions for assembling something, from knowing when comprehension is breaking down to having strategies for figuring out unknown words. We are interested in students becoming more completely well as readers, which means not only having the skills and strategies to read the text, but also enjoying the text, having ideas, and developing identity and agency (Johnston 2004, 2012). When considering our students' growth and progress as readers and the joyful instruction that can support these things, we think about how our students are weaving together all the facets of their reading lives and pause to ask the bigger question, "How well are my students as readers?"

• • • Why We Wrote This Book

In this anxiety-riddled period in educational history, there is extreme pressure to teach the standards and meet demands of accountability. Even as we were working on this book, Kim dealt with the repercussions of New York State's Common Core units of study, which translated into her ten-year-old son (who loves to read) spending his first ten days of school reading nothing but the Universal Declaration of Human Rights (United Nations Office of the High Commissioner for Human Rights 1948) and coming home from school each day talking about how much he hated reading!

As illustrated in the story above about Nathan, accountability pressures can not only lead us to move away from, or in some cases abandon, our highest purposes, but also influence us to teach in ways that actually interfere with the realizations of our highest visions for students. Instead, we would rather teach "in ways that strengthen student-centered, deeply interactive approaches to literacy, approaches that invite students to live richly literate lives, using reading and writing to pursue goals of personal and social significance" (Calkins, Ehrenworth, and Lehman 2012, 2), despite accountability demands. Simply put, we want to show you new ways to address external standards while remaining true to your inner teacher—that is, to *your* standards.

To begin our collaboration with you, we ask you to stop for a moment and consider why you became a teacher in the first place. What is your vision for students as lifelong learners?

When we work with groups of teachers to help them reconnect with their visions for students as lifelong learners, the following ideas repeatedly emerge:

> Lifelong learners are curious.

> Lifelong learners are willing to take risks.

> Lifelong learners need answers to the questions that nag them.

Lifelong learners don't give up when they are trying to figure something out.

Lifelong learners learn for fun and/or relaxation.

Lifelong learners are excited about what they are learning.

Lifelong learners connect ideas.

Lifelong learners think across disciplines.

Lifelong learners aren't afraid to mess up.

Lifelong learners seek differing perspectives.

Lifelong learners see potential for learning in all life's experiences.

This ideal of lifelong "learnership" is much bigger than a school mural or the printed mission statement that administrators require teachers to hang inside their classroom doors. Furthermore, although lifelong learnership includes most of the ideals of "college and career readiness" asserted by the authors of the Common Core (2010), lifelong learning is bigger than preparing students for what happens in college and the workplace; it's about hope and recognizing the classroom as "a location of possibility" (Hooks 1994, 107). These possibilities are what drove many of us to the field of education in the first place; few teachers (if any) would say that they entered the field to raise test scores!

In her book *What Keeps Teachers Going?* in which she explores teacher identities and autobiographies and how these relate to students, Sonia Nieto writes, "Hope is at the very essence of teaching. In all my years of working with teachers, I have found that hope is perhaps the one quality that all good teachers share. Whether they teach in preschool or college, whether they teach math or art, good teachers have an abiding faith" (2003, 53).

Lifelong learning is about tapping into this faith, hope, and possibility and showing students the potential of their minds, and it can change the way we teach.

We wrote *Reading Wellness* because we want to help you find new ways of meeting the demands and pressures of the standards and other account-ability measures while staying connected to your broader visions of students as readers, helping them establish habits that will support a lifetime of reading wellness. Our intent is to offer you practical, self-extending lessons that invite you to think about *your* intent as you teach toward instructional standards, ever mindful of your larger goals for students as readers and people. We want to offer you standards-based actions to try in your classroom, actions that simultaneously stir your thoughts about your ideals, reaching far beyond standards-based instruction.

● ● ● Teaching and Learning Intentionally

As a foundation for our collaboration with you, we offer four equally important "intentions" that run throughout this text as supporting ideas. These intentions inform our work in schools with teachers and students; they shape the thoughts we translate to paper, and they form an evaluative tool against which we can consider our movement toward the best selves *we* want to grow into. Even more, they hold up for us as tenets that students can eventually grow to own. You may use different words or articulate these ideals differently, but in all likelihood, if you are reading this book, these principles already shape your vision for yourself and your students. These intentions hold an element of universality that predated the Common Core State Standards and will certainly live beyond them.

Intention 1: We intend toward alignment with our inner teacher.

In these days of aligning curricula, instruction, and language with performance standards, we offer as our primary teaching intention alignment with our highest purpose for teaching—that is, a focus on lifelong learning. This includes a reconnection with our original visions for our teaching selves and a reawakening of our loftiest visions for students as learners. Staying true to the alignment intention means keeping our sights set on our long-term outcomes and the ways in which our instructional decisions can affect who children will grow up to become. The alignment intention is all about recognizing and acting on our agency as teachers, and using this agency to empower students.

Although alignment of this sort involves recognizing when our instruction has wandered across our internal boundaries to meet standards objectives, it doesn't mean that we are narrow-minded. Rather, alignment to our true teaching selves also involves persistently exploring the counterpoints to what we believe about teaching children. So, we step into our most closely held tenets and assume that we are vulnerable to bias, that we inadvertently tend toward habits that can limit our students, and that we must bravely explore the value of those things that make us bristle.

The reclamation of the term *alignment* as staying true to our inner teacher (versus alignment to standards) lets us claim bodies of research that hold tremendous promise for helping students become lifelong learners, such as Carol Dweck's research on mindset (2006) or the research on the gradual release of responsibility (Burkins and Croft 2010; Pearson and Gallagher 1983), both of which reinforce problem solving rather than dependence and can translate into a lifetime of powerful learning for students while also making our inner teacher happy.

Your work within Intention 1 may involve aligning to deeply felt beliefs that are different from ours. Whether you align yourself to developing classroom community, teaching with authentic literature, integrating cultural relevance, pushing for rigor, teaching children flexible habits of mind, or all of the above, the work begins with identifying the ways of working that are most important for *you*.

To evaluate lessons against the alignment intention, ask yourself the following questions:

- Does my inner teacher, my highest teaching self, feel safe (even happy) in teaching this lesson? How do I know?

- How does this lesson show students their power as learners?

- Am I excited about teaching this lesson? Why?

Intention 2: We intend toward balance.

We intend to balance the aforementioned alignment with expectations set forth by the instructional standards we are required to teach, whether state directives around the Common Core State Standards or district expectations that we use certain curricula. We must attend to accountability demands intentionally, but we want to do so without losing sight of our best selves as educators and who we want students to grow to become. Balancing the expectations of others and our expectations of ourselves is possible, and critical, requiring us to weave moments of alignment between our intentions toward lifelong learnership (which includes learner attributes such as mindset, agency, purpose, and vision) and district, state, and national movements toward some degree of standardization. The balance intention recognizes the role of standards-based/standardized instruction in today's classroom, but always checks standards-based actions against our alignment with ourselves (Intention 1).

Intention 2 not only attends to standards, however, but also deals with the ways we fight our own biases. Whatever we believe about teaching, we must recognize that believing something doesn't necessarily make it best for us or for students. In fact, even though we must take care of our inner teacher (Intention 1), we must also challenge him or her, lest we fall into routines and practices simply because they are comfortable, because they are habituated, or because *not* doing them would suddenly throw all our previous teaching into question.

To evaluate lessons against the balance intention, consider the following questions:

- How well does this lesson help students meet the expectations others place on my students and classroom? How do I know?

- How does this lesson accentuate the aspects of accountability and standardization that are most closely connected to what my inner teacher holds most important?

- How does this lesson marry the goals of my inner teacher, the immediate considerations of accountability, and checks against my own biases?

Intention 3: We intend toward sustainability.

Classroom time restraints demand that we teach lessons that serve purposes beyond the immediate work. Sustainable lessons are those that teach processes, strategies, or routines that will support learning in other contexts. We acknowledge that, ultimately, practices that support reading wellness must be self-sustaining, even habituated. So, we begin not only with the end in mind (Covey 1989), but with the *end in place* as much as is possible. This means that we help students practice their approximations of the targeted, integrated tasks as early in the gradual release as possible (Pearson and Gallagher 1983). Because "the key to remembering is repetition and use" (Fisher and Frey 2009, 19), we must prioritize lessons that teach ways of learning that can grow into other lessons. Thus, the lessons in this book are not an end in themselves, but rather pathways for establishing new ways of being, knowing, and doing that can serve students within our classroom communities, and even for a lifetime. To evaluate lessons against the sustainability intention, consider the following questions:

- How does the core of this lesson make future work easier, better, and deeper?

- How does this lesson make it easier for us, as a classroom community, to talk about our work? For example, does this lesson introduce a classroom vocabulary that will continue to support students?

- How will habituating what they are practicing in this lesson make students more "well" as readers?

Intention 4: We intend toward joy.

We intend toward joyful instruction and joyful learning in classrooms all the time! We actively search for sources of joy, and work to extend and perpetuate them. We are not referring to "fun" lessons or "cute" activities, although joyful learning *is* usually fun and may well lead to inspired (and even inspiring) and innovative student work. *Joy* in this context refers to the moments you and your students are engaged in work that matters to you, that holds the potential for propelling lifelong learning habits, and that results in growth both toward accountability standards and toward an agentive life of learning. To evaluate lessons against the joy intention, consider the following questions:

- What makes this lesson memorable?

- How does this lesson fill my students and me with energy, awe, and/or inspiration?

- How well does this lesson engage students in ways that make them forget they are working?

- How does this lesson teach students to love learning?

It is important to note that there is overlap among the four intentions; they are not categorical, but connected. Consequently, the important work around the intentions is *not* in categorizing lessons into the "correct" intention, but in exploring the ways in which these ideals can weave through our lessons. In sum, our vision for teachers and students is founded on integrating (versus sorting) skills, strategies, and dispositions focused on growth and engagement. We do not claim mastery of these intentions, but commit constant effort to nurturing them, aiming for balance and momentum toward increased wellness.

• • • The Shape of This Book

This book charts a path for helping students develop reading wellness—with an incidental, parallel pathway for extending teacher wellness—that runs through six chapters. *Reading Wellness* integrates a wellness metaphor across all the chapters, with vignettes, discussions, book lists, and lessons designed to help you meet the demands of the external standards while staying in touch with your vision for students as lifelong learners. All the lessons in this book have been field-tested by both of us, in real classrooms with real teachers and students.

Chapter 1, "Love," presents the *Heart, Head, Hands, and Feet* graphic organizer, which we use for interacting with biographies of people who pursued their passions throughout their lifetimes, such as Jane Goodall and Henry Ford. This lesson serves as a springboard for student-directed explorations of informational text, while also introducing much energy and joy to classroom communities.

In Chapter 2, we translate the mindset research into a lesson about "posture," titled *Leaning In/Leaning Out.* After giving students a physical cue for indicating the way attitude affects how they approach a task, this lesson asks students to think about whether they are "leaning in" or "leaning out" when they read complex text. Most important, *Leaning In/Leaning Out* helps students understand that they are in charge of their learning.

Because we see so many students who don't notice when their comprehension is breaking down, in Chapter 3, "Alignment," we introduce a lesson called *Does That Match?,* which helps students consider the ways the print and the meaning of a text work together to support their comprehension. This lesson pushes students to take action when their reading is not "aligned."

Next, in Chapter 4, "Mindfulness," we present the *Deep Breathing* lesson, which connects instruction to the practice of breathing deeply, using this habit as a reminder that close reading is slow, intentional rereading. Based on the idea that deep comprehension requires the reader to be "in the moment," the *Deep Breathing* lesson uses an image to show students how to read slowly and reread complex texts for the purpose of synthesizing them.

The *Lifting Weights* lesson, presented in Chapter 5, takes the idea of matching texts to readers and extends it beyond traditional practices, such as looking for "just right" books or applying the "five-finger" rule. This chapter offers a metaphor for reconceptualizing for students the idea of reading challenging texts, and offers a new paradigm for teaching students to self-select books, including those that are complex and/or challenging.

Finally, we close *Reading Wellness* with Chapter 6, "Joy," which is filled with stories about joyful interactions with texts. Chapter 6 introduces the *Feeling Good* lesson, which encourages students to think about the many different ways in which books give them good feelings. The *Feeling Good* lesson is designed to help students monitor their comprehension while also searching for books and authors they love.

••• Putting It All Together

Before, during, and even after the writing of *Reading Wellness,* we field-tested the lessons we have shared with you here. The testing and refinement continues, even as you read this book. Although each of the *Reading Wellness* lessons can stand alone, we find that their most promising potential rests in the synergistic ways they can work together, with each lesson connecting to the previous one.

In addition, after much trial and error, we have found that the order in which the lessons are presented in this book is an instructionally sound order for implementing them. For example, the *Leaning In/Leaning Out* lesson (Chapter 2) is more effective if students have books about their passions—books selected after participating in the *Heart, Head, Hands, and Feet* lesson (Chapter 1) that they can "lean in" to. Similarly, the *Deep Breathing* lesson (Chapter 4) is easier to teach after the *Does That Match?* lesson (Chapter 3).

We have also found that the lessons are more effective if there is a bit of time to practice the ideas and vocabulary from one lesson before teaching the next. Ideally, teaching one lesson a week, solidifying its concepts through lesson variations and extensions across a week, and then introducing the next lesson a week or so later is ideal. Teaching *Reading Wellness* sequentially across weeks, you will discover the ways in which one lesson's ideas support the next.

For example, during a conference during independent reading after the *Feeling Good* lesson (Chapter 6), one student was trying to figure out the word *Tecumsah.* The teacher naturally referred to previous learning from the *Does That Match?* lesson (Chapter 3), which supported the student in figuring out the word and even experiencing the joy of success. If you and your students own all of these metaphors, pulling them out of your tool kits as you need them, they can serve student independence and proficiency in many, many contexts all year long.

● ● ● Our Vision for You

We want you to read this text knowing that our truth doesn't have to be your truth. By the same token, we invite you to interrogate your thinking as we present ideas that may offer some substantive paradigm shifts. In the end, we want you to take the ideas and lessons in *Reading Wellness* and shape them to your intentions in ways that help you reach your ideals for yourself and for your students, including those that extend far beyond college and career readiness.

We begin this adventure together by asking the obvious question in hopes of reaching beyond *I am well* to your sincerest, reflective response. So, how well *are* you?

Chapter 1

LOVE—AUTHENTIC REASONS TO READ INFORMATIONAL TEXTS CLOSELY

Educating the mind without educating the heart is no education at all.

——ARISTOTLE

It is Sunday afternoon. After four hours of cleaning and laundry, you sink into your couch with the stack of dog-eared student papers you've been carrying around for a week. Your students' scores are due tomorrow. You thumb through the pages of student writing, estimating that it will take you at least two hours to rate them along the state writing rubric. Sipping coffee from your "World's Greatest Teacher" mug, your mind wanders. You think, *Maybe I should get a dog. Maybe walking a dog would be better at waking me up in the afternoon than coffee.* You begin to deliberate over the advantages and disadvantages of particular dog breeds.

Suddenly, realizing your avoidance strategy, you adjust your position on the couch, take up your purple pen, and recommit to reading student papers. Your students wrote these essays in response to the school district's practice writing test, which, despite the label "Informational Prompt," posed the question "If you could trade places with someone, who would it be?" As you begin reading the papers, you realize that many of your students misunderstood the prompt and wrote about the person in the classroom with whom they would literally trade places. Antonio wrote, "I would trade places with Sandra because she sits next to Reginald and he is my best friend." *Good grief!* you mutter to yourself, wondering who at the central office needs clarification on the definition of informational writing.

You manage to focus and dig into your work, despite your disappointment. Just as you hit your grading groove, your own children, the very two you had charged with being quiet while you worked, pull books from a nearby shelf and enjoy them loudly on the floor at your feet. You press on, despite the voice in your head telling you that the writing samples are evidence that you are a bad teacher, and the rowdy, disobedient children now laughing uproariously are simultaneous evidence that you are a bad parent.

Frustrated, you begin to wonder if you need something stronger than coffee as your five-year-old son climbs onto the couch next to you with *The Three Questions* by Jon J. Muth (2002) and asks you to read it to him.

You shake your head as you say, "I'm sorry, I can't right now." You need to finish reading papers, and you know it would take a long time for you to read *The Three Questions*. You would have to explain a lot, and even then your son might not really understand it. You suggest that he turn on the television instead.

He is not dissuaded. Thumbing through the beautiful illustrations, he persists. "What's it about?"

You take a deep breath and try to come up with a summary. "The importance of *now*," you finally say.

"What does that mean?"

You sigh, exasperated. "It's about figuring out what is important, okay? Now I need you to be quiet because I have to work!"

"But you always have to work," he replies.

The two of you look at each other through a several-second pause. Tears well up in your eyes. He is absolutely right, and you both know it. You open the book and begin to read about figuring out what is important, grateful that your children are sometimes wiser than you and realizing that the two of you will have to talk a lot for *you* to really understand the book.

If this story sounds all too familiar to you, it is probably because some version of it is a daily reality for most teachers. This vignette initially presents a tension, for the mother/teacher, between doing what nourishes her (such as exercising or reading aloud to her children) and what needs to be done (such as grading papers, household chores, and so on) and serves as a metaphor for the tension between teaching lifelong learning and teaching curricular standards. Teaching is a delicate balancing act that forces us to reconcile our ideals for fostering lifelong learnership with top-down pressures for accountability. However, the reality is that, very often, our intentions and our actions *don't* line up. In fact, our actions sometimes work against our intentions, which can leave us feeling as if we are doing nothing well.

With each year of the No Child Left Behind era, instruction tended to focus more and more on the immediacy of standardized tests, until there were fewer and fewer time, energy, or money resources for intentionally working toward long-term ideals for students. Many of us have found ourselves working toward test scores while *hoping* toward the visions inscribed upon our hearts. This misalignment affects our general wellness in and out of school, and it can make us feel as if we have fallen out of love with teaching. In moments of reflection and clarity, we look in the mirror and realize that our reality is moving farther and farther away from our original vision, and we wonder how we got here and, more important, how we will find our way back. As in the story that opens this chapter, the tension between our instructional values (lifelong learnership) and systemic pressures is in many ways a false dichotomy; the two perceived "opposing tensions" are not mutually exclusive. It is possible, and critical, to weave moments of balance between intention and necessity into our instruction, giving the term *alignment* new meaning.

In the remainder of this chapter, we work to help you find the common points between your immediate pressures and your larger purposes as a teacher. Next, we introduce the *Heart, Head, Hands, and Feet* lesson structure, which invites students to closely read biographies of passionate people. Then, we present three different *Heart, Head, Hands, and Feet* lessons, using three different texts, and suggest extensions for integrating the lesson structure into other areas of your instruction. Finally, we examine the *Heart, Head, Hands, and Feet* graphic organizer through the lenses of our four intentions: alignment, balance, sustainability, and joy.

●●● Reading Because Someone Else Tells Them To

Walk into many classrooms at the beginning of the school year and you are likely to see, hanging on the walls, evidence of conversations about what readers do. We create *What Readers Do* charts with statements such as these:

> Read a lot.
>
> Look for books by authors we know and love.
>
> Picture the story in our minds.
>
> Read to understand.
>
> Use strategies.

These charts become springboards for conversations with students about setting reading goals. We ask students to consider which items on the *What Readers Do* chart reflect their current reading habits and which ones need their attention. We ask them to formulate a goal for themselves as readers, which they write on index cards cut into the shape of footballs so that we can staple them to a bulletin board with a giant goalpost on it. Their goals include statements such as these:

> Shania: I will read more pages.
>
> Louis: I will read more nonfiction.
>
> Jordan: I will find a quiet place to read so that I won't be so distracted.

And then we continue on with the school year, only to look up one day in November to realize that although Shania is reading a lot, we don't know if she is actually reading *more*. And Louis has barely finished a fiction book, let alone read more nonfiction. We wring our hands and wonder why students rarely realize the goals they set for themselves. Instinctively, we resolve to revisit "what readers do," but perhaps, instead, what we should think about is what drives readers' desire to read.

When we ask what drives reading, inevitably, we begin to think about reading very differently than simply asking "What do readers do?" To help us explore this idea, let's begin by thinking about famed primatologist Jane Goodall. Did she read because she wanted to improve her reading rate or because she wanted to read chapter books? Or was her desire to read motivated by something entirely different?

● ● ● Teaching Children to Read as Jane Goodall Read

It's common knowledge that Jane Goodall loved animals. When Jane was a young girl, she once spent five hours in her grandmother's stuffy henhouse patiently watching the chickens so that she could figure out how eggs are laid. She climbed trees to watch birds and sketched the animals that she saw in her backyard. One might think that young Jane imagined herself becoming a veterinarian or zookeeper or even a farmer; however, that was not the case. When she was ten years old, Jane announced to her family that when she grew up, she would move to Africa to study and write about animals (Bardhan-Quallan 2008). How did a young girl from the English countryside envision such an unusual vocation in such a faraway, exotic place?

Quite simply, Jane Goodall was a reader. She read informational books about the animals in her backyard and about other animals she knew existed but couldn't see every day. She also read stories, such as *Tarzan of the Apes* (Burroughs 1914) and *The Story of Dr. Dolittle* (Lofting 1920). In fact, Dr. Dolittle helped Jane imagine going to Africa to live with animals. And after reading about Tarzan, she knew that she'd make a far better Jane than the one in the story. Jane read not because others set goals for her, but because she was driven by her passions. Her reading was connected to the things she loved.

Unlike so many of our students who read to meet reading-log requirements or to become more fluent, Jane didn't think of reading as an end in itself. Reading was merely a vehicle she used on the path to her dreams. Jane's example suggests that if we are to help children move closer to *our* goals for their improved proficiency, perhaps we need to start with *their* passions, letting reading stamina and reading volume surface as the happy by-products of their self-directed explorations of things they want to do, whether cooking pastries or flying airplanes. These explorations give students opportunities to read themselves into lives and places that stretch their imagination, much like reading *Tarzan of the Apes* influenced Jane Goodall's vision of her future.

We know that helping children become great readers is as much about them seeing themselves as transformative thinkers and people influenced by stories and information as it is about refining their ability to infer or determine the main idea. Finding the balance between alignment with your inner teacher and accountability for external standards will probably require that you also show students the opportunities reading offers them.

••• The *Heart, Head, Hands, and Feet* Lesson Overview

The *Heart, Head, Hands, and Feet* lesson introduces a graphic organizer that shows students their power as learners by teaching them to recognize the connection between passion, mindset, and effort.

A *Heart, Head, Hands, and Feet* lesson begins by engaging students in a close reading of a story with a character who is determined to accomplish a goal. Students identify what the character loves to do (heart). Next, they look for evidence in the text that indicates what the character imagines for his or her future, building out from the driving passion (head). From there, students are invited to read on and/or reread to consider what steps or actions the character takes to realize his or her dream, citing textual evidence for each step or action (hands and feet).

Figure 1.1
Jan hugs a first grader after teaching a *Heart, Head, Hands, and Feet* lesson.

After completing the graphic organizer (Figure 1.2) with the selected text, the teacher models completing the *Heart, Head, Hands, and Feet* graphic organizer by considering his or her own areas of passion and interest. Next, students get to complete their own graphic organizers. Once teachers collect information about student interests, they can gather informational books specific to these interests, offering students complex texts they will work to understand as they continue to read them over the next few days, thinking about their own hearts, heads, hands, and feet. Table 1.1 describes the process for introducing the *Heart, Head, Hands, and Feet* lesson and graphic organizer.

Table 1.1

The *Heart, Head, Hands, and Feet* Lesson

PURPOSE	
LONG-RANGE PURPOSES	IMMEDIATE PURPOSES
• To help students see connections between their actions today and their futures • To show students the ways in which informational texts can serve them	• To teach students to read texts closely to find text-based evidence for statements they make about the main character • To give students authentic reasons for reading complex informational text closely
STANDARDS	TIME FRAME
Reading Anchor Standards: 1, 2, 3, 10	45–60 minutes
MATERIALS	
A suitable biography or autobiography (see list of titles on pages 25–26), chart paper and markers, heart-shaped glasses, copy of graphic organizer (see Appendix A)	

continued

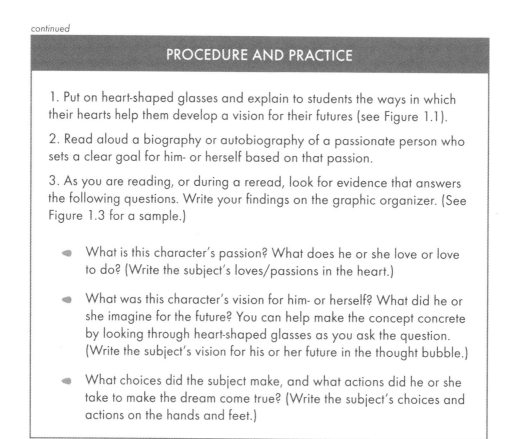

PROCEDURE AND PRACTICE

1. Put on heart-shaped glasses and explain to students the ways in which their hearts help them develop a vision for their futures (see Figure 1.1).

2. Read aloud a biography or autobiography of a passionate person who sets a clear goal for him- or herself based on that passion.

3. As you are reading, or during a reread, look for evidence that answers the following questions. Write your findings on the graphic organizer. (See Figure 1.3 for a sample.)

- What is this character's passion? What does he or she love or love to do? (Write the subject's loves/passions in the heart.)

- What was this character's vision for him- or herself? What did he or she imagine for the future? You can help make the concept concrete by looking through heart-shaped glasses as you ask the question. (Write the subject's vision for his or her future in the thought bubble.)

- What choices did the subject make, and what actions did he or she take to make the dream come true? (Write the subject's choices and actions on the hands and feet.)

••• *Heart, Head, Hands, and Feet* Sample Lessons

A *Heart, Head, Hands, and Feet* lesson begins with selecting an appropriately complex biography, autobiography, or story of an inspiring person who was motivated by a passion (heart), who went on to imagine where this passion could take him or her (head), and who continued to pursue the goal with concrete actions (hands and feet).

Lesson 1: *Me . . . Jane* by Patrick McDonnell

One of our favorite titles for *Heart, Head, Hands, and Feet* is *Me . . . Jane* (McDonnell 2011). In the opening pages of this book, Patrick McDonnell reveals many of Jane Goodall's childhood passions: her stuffed chimpanzee (Jubilee), being outdoors, and animals. Not until the end of the story, however, does it become apparent how Jane's passions are connected to what she imagines for her future.

After reading the book aloud once and helping students make the connection between Jane's childhood passions and what she imagined for her grown-up future, we reread and ask students to note the actions young Jane took to move in the direction of this dream. As students cite evidence, such as Jane observing the chickens in the henhouse and sketching the animals in her backyard, we write their noticings on the hands and feet of the graphic organizer. See Figure 1.2, which presents a completed *Heart, Head, Hands, and Feet* graphic organizer, and Table 1.2, which lists possible graphic organizer content from *Me . . . Jane.*

Figure 1.2
Completed *Heart, Head, Hands, and Feet* Graphic Organizer

Table 1.2

Contents of the *Heart, Head, Hands, and Feet* Graphic Organizer for *Me . . . Jane*

HEART	HEAD	HANDS & FEET
• animals • Jubilee, her stuffed monkey • being outside	• I'm going to go to Africa and study and live with animals!	• Sneak into the henhouse and watch the chickens lay eggs • Read information about animals • Read stories about animals • Sketch the animals in the backyard

Lesson 2: *Fifty Cents and a Dream* by Jabari Asim

Reading lots of books through the lens of *Head, Heart, Hands, and Feet* provides students opportunities to explore topics of interest while continuing to learn how passions and goal attainment are connected. In another *Heart, Head, Hands, and Feet* lesson using Jabari Asim's *Fifty Cents and a Dream* (2012), students notice right away that unlike *Me . . . Jane*, which doesn't reveal Jane Goodall's dream until the end of the book, both Booker T. Washington's passion for learning *and* his life's aspiration—learning to read—are revealed in the opening pages of this book.

As we guide children in their exploration of what Booker's hands and feet did to help him realize this dream, we look carefully at the text through the lens of passion. We notice the words that the author chose, and as we linger with language such as "the strange marks marched and danced across the page, making him smile and laugh with joy," students note the extent of Booker's longing. Table 1.3 identifies some of the elements of the *Heart, Head, Hands, and Feet* graphic organizer as they are presented in *Fifty Cents and a Dream*.

Table 1.3

Contents of the *Heart, Head, Hands, and Feet* Graphic Organizer for *Fifty Cents and a Dream*

HEART	HEAD	HANDS & FEET
• books • letters • words • reading • learning • studying	• I want to learn to read and go to school.	• Touched the covers of books whenever he could • Traced the strange marks in the spelling book his mother got for him • Listened to the stranger from Ohio read aloud the daily news

Lesson 3: *Marie Curie, A Brilliant Life* by Elizabeth MacLeod

Sometimes, we select sections of longer biographies as the subject of our *Heart, Head, Hands, and Feet* study. When using *Marie Curie: A Brilliant Life* (2004) we focus on the section titled "Working Girl" (see Table 1.4). In this section, some of Marie's passions require readers to piece together bits of text to infer what was in her heart ("At one ball, she wore through a new pair of dancing slippers!" and "but Marya kept working for the family because Bronya was depending on her"), whereas other passions, such as her love for Kazmierz, the son of the wealthy family for whom she worked as a governess, are more explicitly stated ("When the oldest boy, Kazmierz, came home from university, he and Marya, now 19, fell in love"). Working to determine how Marie Curie imagined her future based upon what was in her heart forced students to carefully sift through some of the "noise" of the text. When one child said, "She imagines growing up to get married" as he considered what would go into Marie's thought bubble, another boy chimed, "No! She wants to become a scientist!" They noted that although it was interesting that she fell in love with a boy and wasn't allowed to marry him, this text was *really* about her persistence in getting educated.

Table 1.4

Contents of the *Heart, Head, Hands, and Feet* Graphic Organizer for *Marie Curie: A Brilliant Life*

HEART	HEAD	HANDS & FEET
studying	I'm going to go to Paris to study physics.	Study at the "Floating University"
learning		Work as a governess to get money to send my sister to Paris first
dancing		
family		Keep working for Zorawski family even though they won't allow me to marry their son
Kazmierz		
science		Work in the labs at the Warsaw Museum of Industry and Agriculture

● ● ● More Titles for *Heart, Head, Hands, and Feet* Lessons

There are many, many picture book biographies, and even some fiction titles, that lend themselves to *Heart, Head, Hands, and Feet* lessons. We find that these texts work well, even for upper elementary students. We include some of our favorite texts for *Heart, Head, Hands, and Feet* lessons in the list that follows.

Me . . . Jane by Patrick McDonnell (2011)

Amazing Grace by Mary Hoffman (1991)

Balloons Over Broadway: The True Story of the Puppeteer of Macy's Parade by Melissa Sweet (2011)

For the Birds: The Life of Roger Tory Peterson by Peggy Thomas (2011)

My Diary from Here to There by Amada Irma Perez (2009)

A Chair for My Mother by Vera B. Williams (1982)

Snowflake Bentley by Jacqueline Briggs Martin (2009)

Someday by Eileen Spinelli (2007)

Somebody Loves You, Mr. Hatch by Eileen Spinelli (1996)

Salt in His Shoes: Michael Jordan in Pursuit of a Dream by Deloris Jordan with Rosalyn M. Jordan (2003)

Henry Ford: Putting the World on Wheels by Dina El Nabli (2008)

Fifty Cents and a Dream: Young Booker T. Washington by Jabari Asim (2012)

Blockhead: The Life of Fibonacci by Joseph D'Agnese (2010)

On a Beam of Light: A Story of Albert Einstein by Jennifer Berne (2013)

••• More Ways to Use *Heart, Head, Hands, and Feet*

Once you have introduced the *Heart, Head, Hands, and Feet* structure, we recommend that you continue this exploration over several days. In fact, *Heart, Head, Hands, and Feet* can support reading and writing throughout the year. Here are a few ways you can continue and extend student use of this graphic organizer.

Let students explore their own passions.

Once you introduce students to the *Heart, Head, Hands, and Feet* graphic organizer, it is easy to support them in completing it as they think about their own passions and imagine their wonderful futures. (See Appendix A for a reproducible version of the *Heart, Head, Hands, and Feet* graphic organizer.) In Figure 1.3, Jack, a fourth grader, describes the work his hands and feet must do to realize his dream of finding an audience for his videos. Jennifer, also in fourth grade, writes in Figure 1.4 that she wants to be a lead singer in a band—and a famous one at that!

Interestingly, getting children to talk about what they love to do is not difficult. We've yet to encounter a child who doesn't have some sense of what he or she enjoys doing. For the few who are slow to come up with ideas, conversations with classmates can prime the pump. The part of the process that can take a bit more support is helping children understand the many possibilities that can grow from one interest. For example, Anthony, who loved to play with action figures, was excited to learn that he could use that passion to write action/adventure stories, illustrate comic books, or design toys.

Helping children explore the ways in which their passions can shape their futures may seem like a lofty goal, even a distraction, from the accountability pressures that demand our attention. Such work creates the "tension" between lifelong learning goals and standards-based instruction that we described earlier in this chapter. At first, it feels like this "heart work" may not align well with standards-based instruction, but we can't shake the urgency. Fortunately, we don't have to. The Common Core State Standards lend themselves to teaching in ways that further lifelong learning, giving us opportunities to get "all students to meet high standards of education and to provide them with a lifelong education that does not have built-in obsolescence" (Fullan, Hill, and Crévola 2006, 1). After exploring student passions through the lens of *Heart, Head, Hands, and*

Figure 1.3
Jack's *Heart, Head, Hands, and Feet Graphic Organizer*

Figure 1.4
Jennifer's *Heart, Head, Hands, and Feet Graphic Organizer*

Feet, one teacher added conversations about careers to each day's morning meeting, working to show students the tremendous variety of options available for them and motivating them to read about their new interests.

Investigate informational topics.

One of our favorite extensions of *Heart, Head, Hands, and Feet* is bringing in collections of books and/or facilitating trips to the library so that students can gather information about their areas of interest. As they begin to read about the things that energize them, they can refine their visions and revise their *Head, Heart, Hands, and Feet* graphic organizers.

After reading Patrick McDonnell's *Me . . . Jane* (2011) aloud to a group of third-grade students and asking them to think about Jane Goodall's passions and dreams and the actions she took as a little girl to move her in the direction of her dreams, Kim brought in baskets of informational books about topics such as skateboarding, horses, and cooking—things that children had told her they "loved." Kim and the classroom teacher watched as the children eagerly thumbed through the books. Books with titles such as *What Is a Scientist?* (Lehn 1998) got the same "YES!" reaction as the books with covers featuring sports stars such as Kobe Bryant. When Jan did the same lesson in a first-grade classroom, every single child in the class enthusiastically read informational text. They eagerly embraced titles such as *Young Orville and Wilbur Wright: First to Fly* (Woods 1992) and *Tale of a Tadpole* (Wallace 1998), most of which were quite complex for this group of young readers.

As they read over days, or even weeks, let students revisit their graphic organizers and add to or revise them. For example, a child who loves fishing and who imagined (with support) growing up to be an ichthyologist, a marine biologist, a competitive fisherperson, a chef, or an artist who paints pictures of fish can explore which of these options really appeals to her. Through talking, reading, and writing about specifics within each of these areas, a student can eliminate, add to, or refine the possibilities listed in the thought bubble. One student, who originally identified an interest in football, discovered (through reading about Harry Houdini) an interest in magic, and added magic/magician to his original graphic organizer.

The intrinsic energy and excitement that grows from this work teaches us that when we shift the classroom conversation from topics such as reading goals and reading strategies to the topics students are dying to explore, the motivational challenges associated with engaging children in closely reading complex informational text begin to dissolve. Jan watched a pair of struggling first-grade readers tackle a tricky book about chimpanzees because they were inspired to be scientists, "just like Jane Goodall." Their teacher explained,

"When we began the *Heart, Head, Hands, and Feet* graphic organizer, our kids were quite aware of policemen, firefighters, and so on, because they had a community helpers unit in kindergarten. However, having them identify things they loved, we exposed them to gymnastics, trapeze, K9 units, fashion design, veterinary medicine, architecture, and video game design. Students began to read complicated books."

Students naturally integrated and applied a host of reading strategies, simply because they desperately wanted to understand the text. We see this over and over again, as the reading strategies students have been taught, often with limited transfer or integration into their independent reading, begin to find a foothold in children's reading processes.

Where once it felt tangential to talk to students about their dreams for the future, suddenly it feels essential. We believe that if we are to help children move along the continuum of independence and proficiency that makes them "college and career ready," it is not only helpful but necessary to connect to their passions. What better way to launch an academic career in the direction of "college and career readiness" than with conversations about what children love to do?

Connect to informational writing.

After reading extensively about their areas of interest, writing about these areas is a natural next step. Oftentimes, writing informational text is challenging because students must deal with both the new content/information and the new text structure. However, if a student is interested in gymnastics and learns all about the Olympics before the informational writing unit begins, then the writing work becomes much easier. See in Figure 1.5 an excerpt from MeKelle's

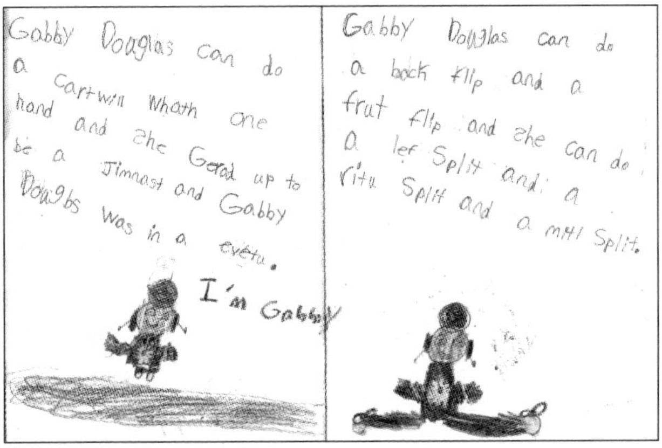

Figure 1.5
First grader MeKelle has written an informational piece about Gabby Douglas.

informational writing about Gabby Douglas, which she developed after exploring her interest in becoming a gymnast. Again, student engagement and motivation become less of an issue when the work arises from student passions.

● ● ● Staying True to Our Intentions

As we mentioned in the introduction of this book, our efforts to be our best teaching selves are driven by four intentions: alignment, balance, sustainability, and joy. In the sections that follow, we use our four intentions to analyze the *Heart, Head, Hands, and Feet* lessons, looking closely at the design and execution of the lesson as well as analyzing the anecdotes and feedback from our experiences teaching them.

Intention 1: We intend toward alignment with our inner teacher.

We believe that most teachers harbor a desire to play an important role in their students' grand plans for their futures. However, aside from asking students, "What do you want to be when you grow up?" we often steer clear of these discussions because they lead to clichéd responses, such as doctor, firefighter, or police officer. Although these are noble and worthy professions, more often than not children say these things not because they love the nature of the job, but because they don't really know what other options the world has to offer them.

The *Heart, Head, Hands, and Feet* lesson expands children's narrow perspectives, moving them beyond their own experiences, just like Jane Goodall. When we read aloud *Me . . . Jane* (McDonnell 2011) to groups of students and turn to the last page, which is a photograph of grown-up Jane reaching out to touch the hand of a baby chimpanzee, a reliable sense of amazement ripples through the classroom. Showing students how a life's work can and should be connected to our passions becomes easy. In addition, the connection between one's actions today and potential future outcomes becomes palpable. Once you use books to connect students' passions to their actions and their power to realize the lives they imagine, we dare you to try to keep them from reading complex informational texts! Awakening passions in students and showing them the power they can access through books makes our inner teacher very happy. When it comes to influencing lifelong learning, what more could a teacher ask?

Another way the *Heart, Head, Hands, and Feet* lesson speaks to our inner teacher is through the ways it builds community. Inevitably, as reading energy builds and students share with each other their individual discoveries, they learn about their classmates' passions. So, their reading becomes a quest not only to learn about the futures they imagine for themselves, but also to help their classmates gather information for their futures. After participating in the *Heart, Head, Hands, and Feet* lesson with Jan, one student brought in pictures of trapeze flyers from the circus he'd attended the night before. He had taken them for a girl in his class who wanted to be an Olympic gymnast but had not considered the trapeze. In these moments, you can see community benefits to individual empowerment, and they can make your inner teacher's jaw drop.

Intention 2: We intend toward balance.

The Common Core's insistence that 50 percent of a child's reading diet include informational text has left some teachers wondering how they will motivate students to read more nonfiction. After a *Heart, Head, Hands, and Feet* lesson with a book such as *Me . . . Jane*, students fight to read different versions of texts about Jane Goodall. Learning that Jane decided to go to Africa because she read about Africa in a book helps them see the possibilities that reading holds for *them*, and they eagerly begin to seek out biographies of people who do the things they love. They also begin to read more about the subject of their interests. In one third-grade classroom, a girl who aspires to be a nurse settled in with Vicki Cobb's *Your Body Battles a Broken Bone* (2008) while a future video game maker settled in with Robin Nelson's *Toys and Games Then and Now* (2003). Motivation becomes intrinsic. They read nonfiction not because there is a standard that says they have to, but because they have an authentic need to do so.

In addition, *Heart, Head, Hands, and Feet* provides students a lens for "reading closely" and "citing specific textual evidence" as required by reading anchor standard 1 (CCSS 2010). However, instead of explicitly and didactically teaching children to read closely, close reading happens naturally as a result of an interesting exploration of successful people. As we teach this lesson in classrooms, we see students reading all the captions under pictures, working to interpret charts and graphs, and making notes of what they are reading, all of which support close reading in integrated and meaningful ways.

Intention 3: We intend toward sustainability.

Because *Heart, Head, Hands, and Feet* is a lens for closely reading texts, students can explore characters, both fictional and real, using this framework across a variety of teaching contexts, such as read-aloud, shared reading, independent reading, partner reading, and so on. After viewing a demonstration of a *Heart, Head, Hands, and Feet* lesson using *Me . . . Jane*, one teacher immediately shared that she couldn't wait to teach the lesson with the picture book *Snowflake Bentley* (Martin 2009). Repeatedly identifying what is in characters' hearts, the things that motivate them, and working to figure out what actions they took to realize this intent helps students deepen their understanding of what they are reading, as well as develop a cumulative appreciation for the time and effort required to attain a goal.

However, the real test of sustainability is how our teaching transfers to students' independent work and thinking. When Kim sat down with Ian, a fourth grader reading Roald Dahl's *The Witches* (1983), she asked him how things were going as a reader. He shared that he didn't get "who was who" in the story. Without prompting, he said, "I know my hands and feet need to do something, but I don't know what!" Although *Heart, Head, Hands, and Feet* had been presented to Ian as a way of closely reading characters and making plans for long-term reading goals, he also saw it as a tool for solving problems. In his mind, when there is a problem, your hands and feet need to spring into action. Kim jumped on his analogy and articulated for him that he had a vision of himself as a reader who works to *really* understand what he is reading, and together they talked about strategies such as adjusting the pace of his reading, rereading confusing parts, and jotting notes like "Bruno = annoying boy who brags a lot" on sticky notes as a way of keeping track of the characters he met in the story.

Most relevant for sustainability, the *Heart, Head, Hands, and Feet* lesson can influence students' reading processes. As teachers across the country work to bridge the gap between where students are and what the CCSS expect of readers, there is little support for the transition between. Most curricula, modules, and units of study available are written for students who are *already* working on the level expected by the standards, students who have presumably had the rigor of the Common Core since they began their school careers as five-year-olds. But in the immediate and very real world of the classroom, there is an implementation disconnect. *Heart, Head, Hands, and Feet* can lure students into work that doesn't feel as much like work, strengthening their reading process via reading volume and giving them opportunities to discover their own capabilities. We have seen students rise to face new challenges, unrelated to their personal passions, because they have realized their own power as readers and discovered their agency.

Intention 4: We intend toward joy.

Because the *Heart, Head, Hands, and Feet* lesson begins by asking kids, "What do you love to do?" it places joy front and center, and their visions for themselves grow out of the things they are passionate about versus the things they think others expect from them. Spending time imagining a wonderful future for yourself is joyful in and of itself, not to mention that it can introduce a completely new paradigm of opportunity for many students.

Sharing baskets of nonfiction texts at the end of the lessons means that *Heart, Head, Hands, and Feet* begins and ends with what students love. Working with students as they consider both the passions and imaginings of successful people as well as their own passions and aspirations for the future is so much fun that we can begin to question whether it is "real" teaching. Fortunately, we have the other intentions to keep joy in check, even though we think unbridled joy in classrooms might be just what students and teachers need. We join Michael Fullan in his call for "irresistibly engaging" learning experiences for students and (brace yourself) for teachers, too (Fullan 2012, 17)!

We have taught this lesson to numerous groups of students, and each time we do, we are swept up in joyful conversations with students and teachers. Students can't wait to dig into the books related to their interests, and they are just as excited when their friends make passionate discoveries. In one third-grade classroom, an aspiring basketball player exclaimed, "Yes!" when he saw a biography about Kobe Bryant, and another boy got equally excited when he found *What Is a Scientist?* (Lehn 1999) for his friend who loves insects.

The lessons are equally joyous for teachers. After participating in a *Heart, Head, Hands, and Feet* lesson, one teacher exclaimed, "You have set my heart on fire!" when she described how excited she was by her students' response. Good teachers, many of whom have felt a barrenness of spirit as they have worked in situations where joy has been drained from classrooms in the name of accountability, find that reclaiming classroom joy can be easier than they thought. Educators have muscle memory for smiling and laughing and looking wide eyed with wonder, and waking up these muscles feels awfully good.

● ● ● Closing Thoughts

From time to time, we as educators must step back and take stock of where we are and, most important, who we are. As we align our instruction with the Common Core standards and standardized assessments, we must remember that we are working toward larger goals of lifelong learning. If we are intentional about aligning our daily instructional choices with our larger beliefs, teaching students to be "independent and proficient" readers gives us the opportunity to synchronize our long- and short-term visions for them.

Heart, Head, Hands, and Feet is an example of a lesson that marries short-range goals for close reading with the belief that lifelong learners set and work to attain their goals. Reading biographies of inspiring people puts children in touch with their own passions and dreams for the future, which gives them authentic reasons to read. When children read to fulfill their own purposes, they not only read closely and carefully, but naturally seek to read informational texts and feel the need to read more—all factors that move them along the continuum of independence and proficiency. When intention and action are in alignment, we spend less energy on resisting what the system dictates and more on ways to make our instruction more fulfilling and invigorating.

● ● ● Questions for Reflection

1. What is your long-term vision for your students? What kind of people do you want them to grow up to be?

2. Think of someone you know who is a quintessential lifelong learner. List this person's characteristics. Now look at your lesson plans for next week. In what ways are you teaching these qualities in your lessons? How can you better integrate them into your lessons?

3. In what ways is your instruction aligned with your vision for students? Where are you out of alignment? Why? What will you do about this?

4. Do you know what you love to do? If so, how can you do more of it? If not, how will you figure out what you love to do?

● ● ● For Further Reading

Why We Teach by Sonia Nieto (2005)

"What Do You Care What Other People Think?" Further Adventures of a Curious Character by Richard Feynman (1988)

Finding Your Own North Star: Claiming the Life You Were Meant to Live by Martha Beck (2001)

The Last Lecture by Randy Pausch (2008)

Chapter 2

POSTURE— MINDSET, AGENCY, AND HARD WORK

The art of love is largely the art of persistence.

—ALBERT ELLIS

After a long Thursday in your third-grade classroom, followed by an excruciatingly long faculty meeting, you load your laptop, your purse, a bag of books, and your six-year-old daughter, Mia (who has her own collection of bags) into the car to head home to tackle homework (yours and hers), dinner, and bedtime. You are fatigued, and your day has been a series of frustrations, from being behind schedule all day, to David's temper tantrum in the middle of math, to the surprise observation from a central office administrator. As you are pulling into traffic, you begin to vent about the irresponsible drivers, the late hour, the fact that the grocery store is going to be crowded, and "Why don't I plan our meals ahead of time, anyway?" Your language gets colorful.

You realize that your daughter is listening, so you take a deep breath and remind yourself of your recent pledge to focus on the positive. Switching back to your more pleasant, mommy voice, you ask the question every parent has asked of every child at the end of every school day since the dawn of time: "How was your day?"

Mia exhales heavily and her shoulders slump as she begins a litany that is remarkably similar to your venting. She describes how she didn't get her morning work finished that morning, how she had to miss part of recess to finish it, how her best friend told her she wasn't her friend anymore, and how her yellow crayon (her favorite color) broke when she was illustrating her story. You take yet another deep breath and let go of the idea that you need to teach her teacher how to teach, that you are worried that Mia will always have trouble making friends, and that you shouldn't have bought the crayons that were on sale.

With some effort, even courage, you choose to say, "You got to illustrate your story today?! I'm so excited for you. You've been working on that piece about Jake [her dog] all week and it has paid off. I am so excited to read your story and see your illustrations! You are becoming such a writer; I can remember when you could barely write your name, and now you are writing stories. Tell me about your illustrations!"

In the rearview mirror you see your daughter smile. She retells the whole story, describing her illustrations in detail. She talks about the hard parts and how she worked at figuring them out, and how she decided what to draw. You tell her that you want to go to school early tomorrow morning so that you can go by her room and let her show it to you. You explain that artists' crayons break all the time, that a crayon breaking means only that she is working hard and getting better, and that you have another yellow one for her at home. She has moved from lost friends and broken crayons to bright yellowness, and you have forgotten about the traffic and have begun to think about how lucky you are to have such a great kid.

♥ ♥ ♥

This vignette captures the struggle many of us experience as we work to change the way we feel by changing the ways we think and talk. The teacher/mother in the preceding story could have taken that moment in a completely different direction, not only making the afternoon even more frustrating for her and her daughter, but also practicing negative patterns of thought that could easily become habituated. Instead, she chose her words intentionally (action), which changed the way she and her daughter felt (emotion). Basically, how well we do work, whether as a mother, a teacher, or even as a student, often depends on how we *feel* about doing the work. Agency begins with believing things are changeable, because if we believe "they can't be changed, taking action is futile" (Johnston 2012, 27).

The recent emphasis on reading "complex" text has spurred a wave of professional conversations about motivating students. Although text complexity includes quantitative, qualitative, and reader and task demands, many educators and publishers define "complex text" as "very, very hard" text, leaving many wondering how we are going to *motivate* students to persevere through such difficult reading (Guthrie 2013). Aside from the obvious need to make sure that texts are *worth* reading, which is a theme throughout this book, and that texts are not skewed beyond complex to downright impossible or inappropriate for students, the issue of "getting" students to persevere often has everything to do with mindset (theirs and ours) and giving them language and habits of thought that help them persist even when the learning becomes very difficult.

• • • Leaning Away from the Water

One of Jan's sons never really learned to swim until he was a teenager. He was always resourceful enough in the water to enjoy himself and keep Jan from worrying, but when he was fourteen, she decided to sign him up for the swim team at the neighborhood pool during the summer. She knew he would learn actual strokes and technique, not to mention how to dive.

Because his skill set was so far below the rest of the swimmers his age and size, Duncan was assigned to the six-to-eight-year-old "guppies" group. Jan wondered if she was doing the right thing, but safety prevailed: she needed to know that he could handle himself in the water when he went to the pool with his friends without her.

Duncan's posture toward swim team was decidedly "leaning away." Although he grudgingly agreed to the arrangement, Jan fielded daily protests, ranging from loud complaints ("It is unfair for you to sign me up to swim early in the morning every day of the summer without even asking me!") to articulate arguments ("Really? Is this the kind of mother you want to be? One who dismisses her son's feelings and opinions?").

One morning, after many mornings of openly resisting swim practice, Duncan got himself out of bed and to the pool without any argument. When he was late returning from practice, Jan created a reason to go to the pool and touch base with the coach. She wondered if Duncan had made it to the pool at all that day or if he was playing swim team hooky. She braced herself for an impending confrontation.

Arriving at the pool, she looked through the fence from afar and was startled to see Duncan in the shallow end with all the other "guppies," most around seven years old, who were offering him advice on his form. The coach couldn't resist Duncan's obvious change in posture, and wandered over to offer him her advice, which he accepted uncharacteristically. The lifeguards and the parent of another swim team member contributed their opinions as well. Duncan listened carefully to everyone. He was not defensive. He didn't shut down when he wasn't successful right away, but asked for clarification. He tried to follow each direction and then checked in for more feedback: "Was that better?" he would ask. And it almost always was.

Within the course of that summer, Duncan progressed from being a resentful and resistant swimmer to embracing swimming. That fall, he joined his high school swim team, and the next summer he earned his lifeguard certification. He spent four summers working as a lifeguard at the public pool, teaching us a valuable lesson about the role mindset plays in motivation, engagement, and posture.

● ● ● Changing Student Learning Postures

In his book *Choice Words* (2004), Peter Johnston describes *agency* as the idea "that if they [students] act, and act strategically, they can accomplish their goals" (29). We think of *posture* as students' attitudinal expressions of agency, or the ways in which they demonstrate a sense of empowerment around a particular task. In this context, posture does not literally refer to the physical position students should assume—i.e., sitting up straight while they are reading. Rather, posture in this context is about considering how students "lean" toward the work: Do they feel defeated without even trying (leaning out), or are they eagerly embracing their work (leaning in)? Since motivation is contingent upon agency, we wonder, how do we show young readers their power? What helped Duncan embrace learning to swim, and how can we replicate this shift in our classrooms, helping students change their posture and embrace learning to read?

When Duncan's summer of swim team began, he said things such as "I'm just not a swimmer" and "My body just isn't built to swim." Children resist reading in much the same way. They say things such as "It's time to read? I hate reading! Reading is boring. Why do we have to read this stuff, anyway?" Though the complaints may differ, the message is the same: "I don't want to do this because I don't think I have what it takes to get better." When faced with reading challenges, many children believe that "good readers" learn to read easily, whereas they themselves were born "bad" at reading. They don't understand the relationship between their persistence and their success; they do not know that they are powerful. They are quick to lean out, and this posture can become habituated.

When this happens, teachers often resort to coaching, cajoling, nudging, cheering, and sometimes coercing; however, a perceived lack of power leaves children feeling as though even their best efforts will change nothing (Dweck 2006; Johnston 2012) or that they have no agency. Until the learner changes his or her mindset, even a talented teacher teaching a beautifully designed lesson will find it difficult to help a child progress along the learning continuum.

Whether children are learning to swim or learning to read, when we think about what shifted with Duncan and what needs to happen in classrooms to change students' feelings of powerlessness, we consider developing student agency a key ingredient. This is characteristically different from motivation, as it is typically incumbent upon the teacher to "motivate" students, whereas agency, which can be fostered (or suppressed) by teachers, comes from within students.

The following structure helps to set the stage for leaning in to challenging work by focusing students' attention on *their* posture toward learning. Participation in a *Leaning In/Leaning Out* lesson teaches students to recognize the effect of their thoughts and words on their actions and emotions, which both instills a sense of agency and gives the classroom community a vocabulary of empowerment.

The *Leaning In/Leaning Out* Lesson Overview

Leaning In/Leaning Out is a metaphor that helps children learn that even when something is hard, they can still learn to do it. It teaches them to "lean in" to challenges and begins with interpreting images that reflect people either resisting or embracing a task. Students start by imagining what these people are thinking. After familiarizing students with the language of "leaning in" (*Oh, yeah!*) and "leaning out" (*Oh, no!*), teachers select a book featuring a character who experiences a wide range of emotions in response to a task or experience. While reading the book aloud, teachers stop at predetermined spots to allow students to consider what the character is thinking at that moment in the story. After analyzing the character's "thought bubble," students look at how positive and negative language and thoughts not only affect the character's emotions and actions, but can influence their own posture toward learning. A complete *Leaning In/Leaning Out* lesson is described in Table 2.1.

Table 2.1

The *Leaning In/Leaning* Out Lesson

PURPOSE	
LONG-RANGE PURPOSES	IMMEDIATE PURPOSE
• To help students understand how language influences thoughts, feelings, and subsequent learning • To show students that they have power over their learning	• To teach students to read texts closely to find text-based evidence to support the inferences they make about characters' thoughts, feelings, and attitudes

continued

STANDARDS	TIME FRAME
Reading Anchor Standards: 1, 2, 3, 4, 10 Language Anchor Standard: 5	45–60 minutes

MATERIALS

Picture book that shows the ways a character leans into or away from a learning experience, images of things children would find appealing or unappealing (birthday cake, swimming pool, getting a shot, homework, etc.)

PROCEDURE AND PRACTICE

1. Begin with a conversation about posture. Talk about how the word *posture* is often used to describe the way a person sits or stands and that during this lesson, you will all be thinking about posture in terms of one's attitude, which can be "leaning in" or "leaning out." When you talk about "leaning in," instruct students to lean forward. When you talk about "leaning out," instruct students to lean back.

2. Show students two or more pictures of things that they are inclined to either like or dislike (cake, snakes, picture books, comic books, etc.). As you share the images, ask students to demonstrate their "posture" toward each one. When they really like what they see, they should lean forward and say "Oh, yeah!" When they dislike what they see, they should lean back and say "Oh, no!" Point out that not everyone feels the same way about each image. Also discuss how a reader might lean out with one image, such as a pile of random picture books, but lean in toward a similar picture, such as a pile of comic books.

3. Next, show students images of people engaging in various tasks— including reading books—some of whom who are obviously happy and others who are not. Ask them to think about what would be written in an imaginary thought bubble above their heads. Be sure students use evidence from the "text," which is the pictures, to support their thinking.

continued

4. Read aloud a story with a character who changes posture, leaning away and leaning into an experience at different points in the story. As the story is read aloud, instruct the students to lean forward or back to indicate that they are tuned in to the character's positive and negative feelings about the experience.

5. After reading, discuss the relationship among the character's mindset, the character's effort, and the outcome related to that effort. Ask students what conclusions this helps them draw about the character's success (or failure). What does this help them understand about how their own mindset can shape the outcome of the things they try?

● ● ● *Leaning In/Leaning Out* Sample Lessons

Leaning In/Leaning Out lessons begin with stories (either fiction or nonfiction) featuring characters who experience a wide range of emotion about the challenges they face. In these books, the character discovers his or her power only after pushing through the inclination to "lean out." It's important to note that, in picture books, the illustrations can offer as much fodder for *Leaning In/Leaning Out* discussions as the text. So, with all these lessons, encourage students to look closely at the illustrations and read the book more than once.

Lesson 1: *Ish* by Peter H. Reynolds

In *Ish* (2004), readers are introduced to Ramon, who loves to draw. When his older brother makes a sarcastic comment about one of his illustrations, Ramon becomes consumed by drawing perfectly, which he finds he is unable to do. Frustrated, Ramon decides to quit drawing altogether. Fortunately, his sister (and biggest fan), Marisol, is standing close by, and Ramon discovers that she has been hanging his rejected drawings on her bedroom wall. Marisol introduces Ramon to the idea of "ish," which rekindles his desire to draw and unleashes an even greater creative spirit. As soon as Ramon "leans in" once again, his artwork becomes better and better, and his enthusiasm begins to spill over into other artistic endeavors. Table 2.2 presents posture examples from *Ish*.

Table 2.2

Changes in Posture Represented in *Ish*

QUOTE FROM BOOK	CHARACTER'S POSTURE
"Ramon loved to draw." (2)	Leaning In
"He kept trying to make his drawings look 'right,' but they never did." (8)	Leaning In *and* Leaning Out
"I'm done." (9)	Leaning Out
"He began to draw what he felt—loose lines." (19)	Leaning In
"He wasn't sure if he was writing poems, but he knew they were poem-ish." (24)	Leaning In

Lesson 2: *Salt in His Shoes* by Deloris Jordan and Roslyn M. Jordan

Much longer than *Ish, Salt in His Shoes* (2003) requires readers to synthesize larger amounts of text to discern when Michael Jordan is "leaning in" and when he is "leaning out." The story begins with Michael going to the neighborhood park with his older brothers to play a game of pickup basketball. Frustrated by being outplayed and teased by a much taller boy on the other team, Michael goes home and asks his mother what he can do to grow taller. He takes her advice to put salt in his shoes and pray, but Michael also begins to spend a lot of time practicing at home. However, in spite of all the effort he puts into practicing, he refuses to go to the park with his brothers, because he knows that he hasn't yet grown. After several months of avoiding the park, he finally agrees to go. When he does, he makes the game-winning shot, which leads him to the surprising discovery that even though he hasn't grown any taller, his practice has helped him grow "better." We present posture examples from *Salt in His Shoes* in Table 2.3.

Table 2.3

Changes in Posture Represented in *Salt in His Shoes*

QUOTE FROM BOOK	CHARACTER'S POSTURE
"Michael loved to play basketball. Every Saturday, he followed his older brothers, Larry and Ronnie, to the park, hoping that they would let him play." (2)	Leaning In
"Growing more excited, Michael twirled around and started asking lots of questions. 'Mama, how long will it take? And how tall do you think I'll get?'" (10)	Leaning In
"When the next Saturday came, his brothers tried to get Michael to go with them to the park, but he wouldn't budge." (19)	Leaning Out
"Feeling more confident than ever, Michael said, 'I'll do it.'" (23)	Leaning In

Lesson 3: *That Book Woman* by Heather Henson

In *That Book Woman* (2008), readers are introduced to Cal, a boy who lives high in the mountains of West Virginia. School and learning to read aren't priorities for Cal, who prefers to plow the fields and herd sheep. Confounded by the woman who regularly braves the elements to bring his family books to read, Cal dismisses her efforts until it occurs to him that there must be a reason she is so persistent. This piques Cal's curiosity, and he decides to try to learn to read. When he does, he discovers that words aren't the "chicken scratch" he first thought. Table 2.4 presents posture examples from *That Book Woman*.

Table 2.4

Changes in Posture Represented in *That Book Woman*

QUOTE FROM BOOK	CHARACTER'S POSTURE
"I was not born to sit so stoney-still a-staring at some chicken scratch." (7)	Leaning Out
"But me, I am no scholar boy." (7)	Leaning Out
"And all at once I yearn to know what makes that Book Woman risk catching cold, or worse." (24)	Leaning In
"I pick a book with words and pictures, too, and hold it out. 'Teach me what it says.'" (25)	Leaning In
"Just chicken scratch, I used to figure, but now I see what's truly there, and I read a little out." (31)	Leaning In

Lesson 4: *Mirette on the High Wire* by Emily Arnold McCully

Mirette on the High Wire (1997), a story about a girl whose mother owns a French boardinghouse frequented by performers in the late nineteenth century, lends an interesting perspective on leaning in and leaning out. Once Mirette sees one of the guests walking on a wire that he set up in the courtyard, she immediately longs to do as he does, and begs him to teach her. He refuses, but she watches and studies his movements from afar and begins to practice when he is not around. In spite of falling many times, Mirette persists. At no point in the story does Mirette lean out, and as a result she becomes more and more skilled at emulating the stranger.

The man soon discovers her ability and begins to coach her. Mirette later learns that the man is the world-renowned tightrope walker Bellini, who is now so stifled by fear, he is unable to perform. When an agent from London discovers that Bellini is staying at the boardinghouse, he persuades Bellini to perform again, and Bellini agrees. However, once on the tightrope, he freezes. With the coaxing of his young friend, who reminds him of the power of persistence, Bellini overcomes his fear and rediscovers the passion that drove him to become an entertainer. Posture examples from *Mirette on the High Wire* are presented in Table 2.5.

Table 2.5

Changes in Posture Represented in *Mirette on the High Wire*

QUOTE FROM BOOK	CHARACTER'S POSTURE
"Mirette worked up the courage to speak. 'Excuse me, Monsieur Bellini, I want to learn to do that!' she cried." (7)	Leaning In
"Finally, after a week of many, many falls, she walked the length of the wire." (10)	Leaning In

continued

"'Once you have fear on the wire, it never leaves,' Bellini said. "'But you must make it leave!' Mirette insisted. "'I cannot,' said Bellini." (18)	Leaning In *and* Leaning Out
"As for the master and his pupil, they were thinking only of the wire, and of crossing to the end." (28)	Leaning In

● ● ● More Titles for *Leaning In/Leaning Out* Lessons

There are many great books that illustrate the ways leaning in to a task makes the work more successful. In addition, some titles illuminate what it means to lean in or lean out, showing the ways in which a character's attitude influences him or her. Some examples include the following:

Space Cat by Jeff Dinardo (2010)

Stand Tall, Molly Lou Melon by Patty Lovell (2001)

The Incredible Book Eating Boy by Oliver Jeffers (2007)

Alexander and the Terrible, Horrible, No Good, Very Bad Day by Judith Viorst (1987)

Amazing Grace by Mary Hoffman (1991)

Chrysanthemum by Kevin Henkes (2008)

Are You Ready to Play Outside? by Mo Willems (2010)

Good News, Bad News by Jeff Mack (2012)

Pete the Cat by Eric Litwin (2011)

Wilma Unlimited: How Wilma Rudolph Became the World's Fastest Woman by Kathleen Krull (2000)

Crickwing by Janell Cannon (2005)

The Big Orange Splot by Daniel Manus Pinkwater (1993)

Lilly's Purple Plastic Purse by Kevin Henkes (2006)

Crow Boy by Taro Yashima (1976)

Learning to Fly by Sebastian Meschenmoser (2013)

In English, of Course by Josephine Nobisso (2002)

● ● ● More Ways to Use the *Leaning In/ Leaning Out* Vocabulary

Once students learn the *Leaning In/Leaning Out* vocabulary, they can use it to support themselves in any learning endeavor. *Leaning In/Leaning Out* is perhaps the most versatile metaphor in this book. Here are a few more ideas for teaching about or with the *Leaning In/Leaning Out* vocabulary.

Create a posture scenario.

We often initiate posture conversations by drawing two stick figures on the board. We name them Chris and Alex, and draw speech bubbles above each character's head. Careful to avoid any gender-specific language, we offer students the following learning scenario that is *not* related to literacy instruction. We read the following story, which uses a math example, all the while drawing the stick figures and their respective thought bubbles on the board as we are telling the story.

Chris and Alex have equal ability in math. Neither is better at math than the other. One day, their teacher gives them a really hard math problem. They both look at the problem and see that it is really difficult.

Chris looks at the math problem and says, "This is hard. I can't do it. I quit." Because Chris doesn't try—not because of a lack of math skill—Chris does not figure out the problem. So, Chris does not learn anything. Now Chris knows a little less math than Alex, even though at the beginning of the math lesson, their math knowledge was the same. Plus, Chris feels disappointed and discouraged about math now. After this happens several times, Chris begins to think, I'm not very good at math. *This means that Chris is even less confident the next time there is a hard math problem. What will happen if Chris keeps leaning out?*

Alex, on the other hand, keeps trying to find the answer to the hard math problem. Because Alex tries to understand—not because of any extra math skill—Alex figures out the problem. This means that Alex learns something. Now Alex knows a little more math than Chris, even though at the beginning of the math lesson, their math knowledge was the same. Plus, Alex feels successful and excited about math. After this happens several times, Alex begins to think, I'm good at math, *which makes Alex more confident the next time there is a hard math problem. What will happen if Alex keeps leaning in?*

Once you read this scenario to students, you can ask them to write about what Chris and Alex are thinking before, during, and after seeing the math lesson. Students can also predict what will happen to these two students. Interestingly, while we are presenting the scenario, we do not refer to Chris and Alex by a specific gender. The students, however, tend to assign them. More often than not, girls will make both Chris and Alex female, whereas boys will do the opposite.

After hearing and writing about this story, students often begin to understand the power of the self-fulfilling prophecies that can accompany leaning-in and leaning-out postures. Writing in response to an earlier version of the story, which had Ivan (leaning in) and Tina (leaning out)—and unintended gender implications, which led to changing the names to Chris and Alex—one student wrote, "Ivan will learn from his mistakes, while Tina isn't learning at all." The writing sample in Figure 2.1 illustrates Devin's grasp of this posture dynamic.

Read characters through the lens of *Leaning In/Leaning Out*.

You can use the *Leaning In/Leaning Out* vocabulary as a tool to help children infer what's inside characters' heads in many instructional contexts, including read-aloud, shared reading, and guided reading. Characters who illustrate leaning-in or leaning-out postures are in abundance in texts. You can create running lists on charts in classrooms as you analyze characters during read-aloud. During independent reading, students can use sticky notes to indicate when a character is leaning in or leaning out. Table 2.6 lists titles with characters who are leaning in and/or leaning out, as well as an illustrative quote from each text.

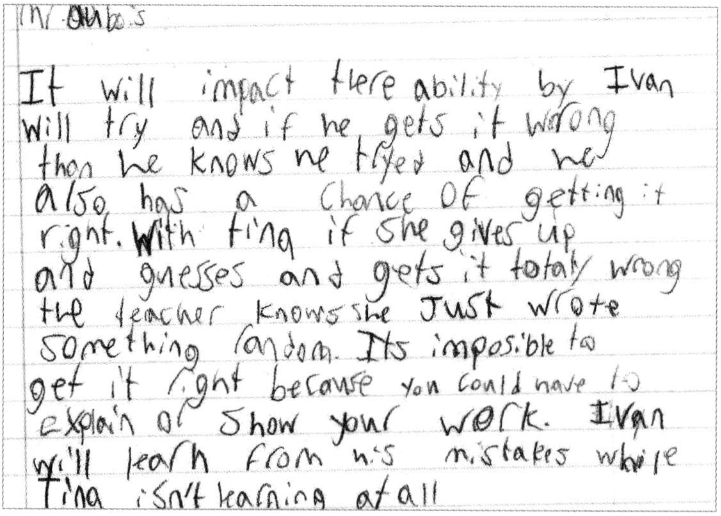

Figure 2.1

Fifth-grade student Devin thinks about the effects of leaning in.

In Class
It will impact there ability by Ivan will try and if he gets it wrong then he knows he tryed and he also has a chance of getting it right. With tina if she gives up and guesses and gets it totaly wrong the teacher knows she Just wrote something random. Its imposible to get it right because you could have to explain or show your work. Ivan will learn from his mistakes while tina isn't karning at all

Table 2.6

Sample Chart of Characters Who Lean In and Lean Out

BOOK TITLE	TEXT	CHARACTER POSTURE
Can I Play Too? by Mo Willems (2010)	The snake asks to play with Gerald and Piggie. They debate whether a snake can play catch. Snake says, "But I can try." (27)	Leaning In
Days with Frog and Toad by Arnold Lobel (1979)	"'Toad, you are right,' said Frog. 'It is a mess.' Toad pulled the covers over his head. 'I will do it tomorrow,' said Toad." (4)	Leaning Out
Henry and Mudge and the Tumbling Trip by Cynthia Rylant (2005)	"Henry had lots of comic books and crossword puzzles to keep him busy on the trip." (14)	Leaning In
Junie B. Jones and a Little Monkey Business by Barbara Park (1993)	Junie finds out her mom is pregnant. "'Babies smell like P.U.,' I explained. 'I smelled one at my friend Grace's house. It had some spit-up on its front. And so I held my nose and hollered, "P.U.! WHAT A STINK BOMB!" And then that Grace made me go home.'" (6)	Leaning Out

continued

Hatchet by Gary Paulsen (1987)	"Brian found it was a long way from sparks to fire. Clearly there had to be something for the sparks to ignite, some kind of tinder or kindling—but what? He brought some dried grass in, tapped sparks into it and watched them die. He tried small twigs, breaking them into little pieces, but that was worse than the grass. Then he tried a combination of the two, grass and twigs." (87)	Leaning In

The more students practice recognizing leaning-in and leaning-out postures in books, the more they will understand the concept and claim the vocabulary as their own. This understanding can lead to them recognizing their own tendencies toward leaning in or leaning out, which we address in the next lesson extension.

Model and teach *Leaning In* language.

Teaching students to lean in to difficult work begins with rethinking how we respond to their efforts to participate in classroom learning. It also involves scaffolding less often but more intentionally, so that students have opportunities to face challenges successfully. Finally, we can recognize their success (especially when the success is choosing not to give up immediately) by saying things that acknowledge their effort instead of making statements such as "Wow! You are so smart; you got that right!" Table 2.7 offers language for teachers to use to develop student agency and independence.

Table 2.7

Leaning In/Leaning Out Language for Teachers

LANGUAGE THAT ENCOURAGES LEANING OUT	LANGUAGE THAT ENCOURAGES LEANING IN
You got it right!	How did you figure that out?
You are so smart.	You really stuck with that. What worked for you and what didn't?
Raise your hand if you have a problem.	Raise your hand when you solve a problem. I want to hear how you figured it out.
At the end of reading workshop, be prepared to share an example of figurative language.	At the end of reading workshop, be prepared to share a tricky spot you encountered in your reading and how you solved your problem.
Let me show you how to figure that out.	I see how hard you are working. You haven't figured it out yet, but I'm sure you will.
Good job!	You are getting better and better at that. What do you know now that you didn't know before?

Whereas Table 2.7 offers teacher language with which you can support students as they begin to lean in to learning more and more, Table 2.8 presents language for students. You can integrate the posture vocabulary into your classroom more deeply by giving students words that support leaning forward. Explicitly teaching these phrases, writing them on charts in the classroom, and helping children notice when they are or are not using language that helps them lean in can help students tune in to their postures.

Table 2.8

Leaning In/Leaning Out Language for Students

STUDENT *LEANING OUT* LANGUAGE	STUDENT *LEANING IN* LANGUAGE
I can't do it.	I can't do it yet.
I'm stuck.	What can I try?
I need help.	What can I do to figure this out? Is there a chart in the room that can help me?
I did it; I'm smart.	I did it; I worked hard.
I did a good job because I got the answer right.	I did a good job because I worked hard and didn't quit.

Of course, there are qualifications for using agentive language. We do not intend for you to eliminate all scaffolding of students or refuse to help them when they are very frustrated. Nor do we want you to simply put extremely difficult text in front of students, use agentive language, and expect them to figure out the text without support. There is a fine balance between helping students develop agency and frustrating them to the point of distress, and we expect you to listen carefully to your inner teacher as you make judgments about how to support them.

• • • Staying True to Our Intentions

Here we consider the ways the *Leaning In/Leaning Out* lesson addresses each of our four intentions: alignment, balance, sustainability, and joy.

Intention 1: We intend toward alignment with our inner teacher.

The grown-ups we know who embody lifelong learning make leaning in a habit. Their posture is decidedly forward, and they are constantly exploring new ideas. When they go to the grocery store, they marvel at new, exotic fruit in the produce section and talk to the produce manager about where it came from. They build inventions in their garages, use YouTube to teach themselves how to play the ukulele, and read all the signage beside the paintings at the museum. If lifelong learners are quick to lean in to new learning, then our reflections around the alignment intention must explore whether we see evidence today that students are growing into such curious, creative, and agentive adults.

The *Leaning In/Leaning Out* vocabulary offers children a metaphor and a process that can support them as they learn to see hard work not as a barrier, but as an opportunity. In the same way that adults grapple with negative feelings about onerous items on their to-do lists, children often lean away from reading because they categorize it with cleaning up their rooms or raking the yard, consider the task mentally challenging, or both. *Leaning In/Leaning Out* teaches children to recognize the correlation between mindset and success, introducing them to the idea that if they expect tasks to be "too hard," then they become even harder! While reading *Ish,* one third grader carefully studied the pictures Ramon drew as he began to lean in to drawing again. Mesmerized, she exclaimed, "Wow! Look at his pictures! They're getting so much better!" Seeing the connection between effort and success is powerful and inevitably helps children begin to think about their own experiences.

Lucas, a fifth-grade boy who uses a loom to make woven bracelets, shared how one particular bracelet design requires a sophisticated weave. He explained that it's difficult to weave the intricate pattern and that he often wants to quit because he frequently messes up. He persists, however, because he is able to make something that is unique, which makes him proud. This persistence has made him better at weaving overall and more confident about tackling the next complex bracelet pattern. More important, thinking aloud about his posture toward weaving and his related success with the bracelets shaped his approach to a complex text he read later in the lesson. Ramon's posture toward drawing informs students' reflections on their learning in areas that interest them, such as weaving, which can then connect to working through a complex text. *Leaning*

In/Leaning Out primes children to embrace cognitively challenging work and teaches them a mindset that not only can serve them in school, but also has the potential to support them their entire learning lives.

The counterpoint to leaning in, leaning out often resonates just as powerfully for children. That is, if you decide you *can't* do something and you lean out, you won't ever get good at it, which creates a self-fulfilling prophecy. Children quickly see that just because you aren't good at something today doesn't mean you can't learn to be good at it, and that if you don't stumble through those initial uncomfortable learning moments when a skill is new, you rob yourself of the opportunity to be "good" at it.

When one fifth-grade student, Laura, said she couldn't come up with ten items on the list of understandings she was supposed to generate from a shared text, Kim asked, "Are you leaning in or leaning out?" She admitted she was leaning out. When Kim asked what was going to happen if she *kept* leaning out, she said she would *really* "get dumb." After the conversation, her posture changed dramatically. She leaned in to the work and was visibly excited about what she was figuring out. At the end of the lesson, she had a substantive list of understandings and a strengthened sense of agency.

Leaning In/Leaning Out debunks for children the myth that we are born with innate skills at reading, writing, music, and so on, and shows them how to live as lifelong learners, starting now. As children lean in to new tasks, and as they are supported in metacognitively recognizing the ways their posture contributed to their success, we see classrooms filled with spontaneous celebrations as they realize success in increasingly difficult work and recognize their own power. Of course, our inner teachers love this.

Intention 2: We intend toward balance.

One of the biggest challenges of implementing the Common Core is that, in the various modules and curricula schools are implementing to lift the difficulty level of the texts students encounter, there are no plans for transition years. The curricula all presume that the students have been taught the content of the previous years. This is the age-old challenge of curricular change, but with the Common Core it is particularly difficult as the shift in text complexity exacts an additional demand on students and teachers.

Anchor standard 10, which requires that students develop proficiency and independence in complex text, is virtually impossible to meet if students are resistant, frustrated, or angry. Thus, the *Leaning In/Leaning Out* vocabulary and its related contributions to students' posture can translate into increased learning, proficiency, and independence, i.e., success with standard 10. The Common Core's focus on processes rather than content requires that we attend to *students'* processes—and students are ultimately in control of those processes, not us. Much like the horse led to water, students can't be forced to engage in the work (that only they can do) of developing independence and proficiency.

After participating in the *Leaning In/Leaning Out* lesson, Jan watched one struggling first grader, James, independently work his way through a Level C text about chimpanzees, employing a host of strategies—from checking the alphabet chart to looking at picture cues to flipping back—as he tackled each obstacle the text presented him. Travon, the boy sitting next to James, sought out the teacher to show her how James was leaning in, and James's classmates, one by one, noticed his posture, his success, and the connection between the two. Travon was so inspired that he found a copy of the book about chimpanzees, and with startlingly intuitive scaffolding from James, worked his way through the text, leaning in all the way. Similarly, a third grader, Brittany, surprised herself by figuring out the meaning of the word *longingly* by leaning in and using context clues rather than relying on the teacher.

In classrooms where discussions about learning posture are central to the energy and work of the learning community, teacher conferences can become celebrations of triumph, which are a form of contagion and are, in our opinion, a powerful path to student success with complex text. Classroom conversations about learning posture can help students notice and connect details in ways that at times feel uncanny. Once students participate in a *Leaning In/Leaning Out* lesson with a book—say, *Ish,* for example—they naturally begin to notice when characters in other books lean in or lean out. Spontaneous eruptions of "Oh, yeah!" and "Oh, no!" serve to verify both that students understand the concept of learning posture and that they are sensitive to it in contexts beyond the original book. And what's more, students often emerge with the powerful understanding that mindset affects achievement and that subsequently, achievement is a choice that is often up to them.

Intention 3: We intend toward sustainability.

The simplicity of the posture metaphor makes it easy for even the youngest students to grasp it quickly, and its broad applicability means that it is useful in almost any learning context, from an eighth grader solving a math problem to a kindergartner learning to tie shoelaces. This generalizability is the very definition of sustainability for us. Of the six lessons we share in this book, *Leaning In/Leaning Out* has proved to be easy to teach and easy to apply widely, and is, consequently, the lesson we think best addresses the sustainability intention.

The metaphor is instantly applicable. For example, near the end of *Ish,* Peter Reynolds writes, "Instead, [Ramon] simply savored it." Once when she was teaching the lesson, a student named Michelle stopped Kim as she read to ask what *savored* meant. Seizing an opportunity to test how much Michelle had internalized about learning postures, Kim asked, "Do you think you can figure it out?"

Michelle replied decisively and promptly: "No."

"Are you leaning in or leaning out, Michelle?" Kim asked.

All eyes turned toward Michelle, who sheepishly admitted that she was leaning out. With the help of her peers, who rallied around her as she considered the illustrations and context clues, Michelle figured out an approximate definition of the word *savored* because she leaned in to it. What's more, her classmates saw the way in which her posture influenced her success.

Obviously we can't promise such teachable moments every time you work with the *Leaning In/Leaning Out* vocabulary, but when it comes to meeting challenges, asking, "Are you leaning in or leaning out?" serves as a simple reminder of all that can happen when students say "Oh, yeah!" instead of "Oh, no!"

Teachers tell us that the *Leaning In/Leaning Out* vocabulary has seeped beyond reading lessons into math lessons, science lessons, and more. In one first-grade classroom, as students transitioned from a reading lesson into a math lesson, Jan talked with Dante, who, during a *Heart, Head, Hands, and Feet* lesson, had expressed his interest in becoming a toy designer. Jan explained to Dante that learning math was very important for him as he prepared for his work designing toys. Dante said he wasn't very good at math. When Jan asked him if he was leaning in or leaning out, he admitted that he was leaning out. Jan went on to explain that he needed to lean in to math, not because his teacher wanted him to learn math, or even because math was a good thing to learn. She told him that he needed to lean in to math because he wanted to be a toy designer, and that doing his math problems was toy designer work. Once he got this connection, his posture totally shifted: he recognized both an authentic purpose for learning math and how he was in charge of preparing to be a toy designer.

Just as powerfully, teachers are reflecting on the ways *they* are leaning in to or away from curricular changes, difficult students, and new principals, and this metacognitive process is influencing them to see the ways in which they are powerful rather than helpless. One teacher wrote, "I can't say enough about how I appreciated those lessons, and their impact on the children and myself." She went on to explain that on the previous day, she had been trying to teach the students a difficult strategy:

> *Yesterday, we were doing the RACE strategy [Read, Answer, Cite Evidence] . . . oh my goodness. It was rough. Then a thought came to my mind . . . LEAN IN TO YOUR PROBLEMS! That's what I told my kids in the midst of a stern talk about effort and challenging tasks. I changed plans for the rest of the day, found a tried and true, loved mentor text from* True Tales of Animal Heroes*, reread a portion I knew they had a copy of, and we practiced RACE together. Then we had an "I wish" reflection discussion and wow . . . what a different group of children on that second go around and what a fantastic discussion.*

Over and over we have watched the *Leaning In/Leaning Out* lesson energize young readers and their teachers, and it is so exciting that we can't help but let the vernacular seep into every other part of our lives. At home, we remind ourselves to lean in to household tasks and our children to lean in to their homework. In terms of sustainability, in fact, we will not be surprised if our sons one day tell their children to "lean in."

Intention 4: We intend toward joy.

Joy is not simply about having fun, but is also about the exhilaration that comes from leaning in to something difficult and discovering our power. One consistent illustration of children understanding the joy that can be found in engaging work comes from their reactions to the images we show them at the beginning of the lesson. The last image we use is of a child reading a book. The child in the picture isn't smiling. He is obviously working hard. When we ask students to lean in or out to show how they think the student in the image feels about the task, they almost always lean in. When we press them, pointing out that the child seems to be working really hard, they articulate that the boy in the picture wants to read the book, so he is willing to work hard. They go on to say that once he figures it out, he will "feel really good" or "he'll be happy" or "he'll feel proud." So our goal becomes helping children translate the rather theoretical connections many of them make between joy and work into something they believe enough to risk leaning in when facing a challenging situation.

We developed the *Leaning In/Leaning Out* vocabulary to help children learn to love learning for its own sake, and we have seen powerful responses from students and teachers. In one fourth-grade classroom, a group of three students grappled with *Henry Ford: Putting the World on Wheels* (El Nabli 2008). After declaring that they were "leaning in" to the difficult text, they decided to focus on figuring out how Henry Ford's passions and aspirations connected to his actions, setting their own purposes for their reading. Throughout the task, they read and reread, eagerly looking back in the text and discussing how one line from the story connected to another. They were energized by their insights, noticing the ways ideas fit together, and they expressed awe at how their learning was related to their posture. In fact, they forgot they were working, and the lesson ended, as we all wish every reading lesson would end, with students disappointed that reading time was over "already."

In looking closely at language, this lesson offers the potential for students to consider in nonthreatening ways the words they use around their learning. Noticing Ramon getting down on himself and feeling that his pictures stink provides readers with a mirror in which to reflect on their own language choices and hence, feelings and actions. Not only is it fun to see where we are acting like Ramon at the beginning of the book, but it is also easy to remember stories and see the parallels between the people we meet in books and our own lives.

●●● Closing Thoughts

The Common Core's call for students to read increasingly complex text has shed an important light on motivating students to embrace hard work. As we think about how to get students to interact with harder texts, we must resist our urge to teach only skills and strategies. Such a focus "results in them knowing strategies, but not necessarily in their acting strategically and having a sense of agency" (Johnston 2004, 31). This means that in addition to explicitly teaching skills and strategies, we must also teach children to think differently about themselves and their work. Although this begins with changing the ways we talk to them, much the way the mother in the opening vignette redirected the course of her afternoon by changing the way she talked to her daughter, it also means helping students experience the power of language through story so that they can begin to see the effect of their words on their feelings and actions. Without a sense of agency, a leaning-in posture, even the best teachers teaching the best lessons will experience difficulty moving students along the proficiency continuum.

●●● Questions for Reflection

1. How do you respond to your students when they answer a question correctly? Does your language emphasize intelligence or ability, or do you praise their efforts?

2. What phrases do you hear yourself saying repeatedly? Does this language help students lean in or lean away from the work they are doing?

3. Think about a lesson you taught that really engaged students. What made the lesson so engaging?

4. What personal challenges are you leaning in to right now? What challenges are you leaning away from?

● ● ● For Further Reading

Choice Words: How Our Language Affects Children's Learning by Peter H. Johnston (2004)

The Inner Game of Tennis: The Classic Guide to the Mental Side of Peak Performance by W. Timothy Galloway (1997)

Happiness Advantage: The Seven Principles of Positive Psychology That Fuel Success and Performance at Work by Shawn Achor (2010)

A Whole New Mind: Why Right-Brainers Will Rule the Future by Daniel Pink (2006)

Outliers: The Story of Success by Malcom Gladwell (2011)

Chapter 3

ALIGNMENT—WORKING TO MAKE SENSE OF THE WORDS

We read a line, a word that lifts us; we rise into a
succession of thoughts that is better than the book.

—RALPH WALDO EMERSON

After an incredibly long week filled with parent conferences, report cards, a faculty meeting, and an assembly on drug prevention, you find yourself at your dining room table on Saturday afternoon surrounded by all the components of your school district's new writing program.

After you randomly fumble through the 200-plus pages of the teacher's guide for more than an hour, you feel fatigued, and only slightly more familiar with the program. You glance out the window, and as your garden catches your eye, you remember that you had intended to plant winter vegetables over the weekend. But even though the lure of playing in the dirt is usually compelling for you, you are surprised to notice that you are no more interested in planting than in reading the teacher's guide spread before you. You take a deep breath, realizing that this fatigue is not new. You've been perpetually tired for a couple of weeks now, and this sudden noticing causes you another layer of anxiety. At some point, you stopped taking care of yourself.

Making a conscious choice to tend less to your professional needs and more to your personal ones, you close the teacher's guide and force yourself to the garage. You gather gardening supplies—a trowel, a twenty-pound bag of soil, a flat of young plants—and walk to the raised beds, each filled with summer's spent plants. By sheer force of will, you pull on your gardening gloves, feeling each finger fill its assigned slot. With decided focus, you fall to your knees and plunge your trowel into the loose dirt, simultaneously scooping soil with your other hand.

Even through your gloves, you feel the cool, moist dirt, and with a wave of energy, you pull off your gloves finger by finger, set down your trowel, and begin to dig with your bare hands. Immediately, you breathe more deeply, and with each handful of dirt and each seedling gently planted, you feel better. A few hours later, the neglected garden is looking loved again. There is dirt under your fingernails, and you have become fully relaxed and joyful. When your thoughts occasionally return to the neglected teacher's guide, instead of feeling guilty, you simply feel pleased that you noticed your need to play in the dirt.

That night, after washing off the garden and putting on your soft pajamas, you set the kitchen timer for thirty minutes and revisit the teacher's guide, which is still waiting where you left it on the dining room table. *I'll learn what I can in half an hour and then I will stop*, you say to yourself decidedly. You honor these boundaries, working hard for just thirty minutes but still learning much more than you did in the hour you spent trying to study the new writing program that morning. When the timer dings, you are pleased at the way you have managed to coordinate the competing demands of your day. You close the writing program and move to the couch, where your partner, who is eating popcorn and watching a movie, is glad you found the time.

Between doctor's appointments and faculty meetings, planning meals and planning lessons, paying bills and paying attention to our significant others, we spend our lives trying to bridge the gap between our day-to-day actions and our visions of our best selves. Maintaining the balance we desire doesn't usually happen unless we are vigilant about reflecting on the quality of our lives: What feels right? What feels wrong? What am I going to do to fix that?

A similar tension exists for readers. Working to negotiate the relationship between print and meaning, readers constantly ask the same quality-control questions: "What feels right?" "What feels wrong? What am I going to do to fix that?" However, like our quality of life, which suffers without constant attention to the ways in which we manage competing demands, the quality of our reading suffers, too.

The Reading Puzzle

Even as you read this, reading specialists and academicians are somewhere debating the roles of print and meaning in a reader's reading process. To us, this is a little like arguing about what is most important when you put together a puzzle: the pieces or the picture itself. The simple answer to the question "Which is more important?" is . . . both!

We absolutely believe that the purpose of reading is to construct meaning (Rosenblatt 2004), just as we deeply understand that one of the essential building blocks in this construction is the print. For us, the important idea is that the letters on the page and the meaning that readers make from them are inextricably linked. In a basic sense, reading is about making the print and the meaning align. This work of alignment is, by definition, at the core of every reader's reading process, even though the nuances of these processes vary from reader to reader.

To illustrate how readers work to align print and meaning, we offer you the following excerpt from *Sleep Like a Tiger* by Mary Logue (2012). You will notice that a few words have been encrypted with Wingdings font. As you work to figure out the encrypted words, think metacognitively and jot down the print and meaning strategies you use.

> *Once there was a little girl who didn't want to go to ♌♏♎ even though the ⬩◆■ had gone away. She told her mother, "I'm not ◆♓❑♏♎."* (1–3)

As you puzzled through the encrypted words, you had to look closely at the print and think deeply about the meaning. Most important, your work was to figure out how these two pieces of information—print and meaning—work together in the text.

• • • When Reading Processes Are Out of Alignment

Efficient readers are equally proficient with the meaning and with the print, and use each to gain insight into the other, checking and cross-checking (Burkins and Croft 2010). Whether a reader is catching a miscue on a particular word or is reading accurately and with understanding, self-monitoring is ongoing for proficient readers. However, too often, the readers we encounter in classrooms are not bringing these two sources of information—print and meaning—into alignment. Instead, they favor one system over another even when their reading inaccurately represents the print on the page or compromises the meaning of the text.

Even proficient readers make miscues or misunderstand text. These hiccups are normal, even healthy. It is patterns of misalignment in reading that concern us. Consider Charles, a fourth-grade reader who encountered the word *elocution* as he read the following passage from the biography *Abraham Lincoln: Lawyer, Leader, Legend* by Justine and Ron Fontes (2001).

> *Abe was working hard to be someone important.*
> *He convinced the town's schoolmaster to teach him*
> *grammar and* elocution, *the art of speaking clearly.*
> *Abe joined the New Salem Debating Society to learn*
> *the proper way to present his opinions. He studied*
> *law, politics, and history as he always had—in stolen*
> *moments, whenever he could.* (17)

Looking at particular print cues and tapping into vocabulary he learned in a recent science lesson about bats, Charles said "echolocation" for *elocution*. If Charles had been thinking about the meaning of the text, he would have quickly realized that echolocation doesn't make sense in this text about Abraham Lincoln. Perhaps he would have then looked more closely at the print, corrected his miscue, and brought his print and meaning into alignment. However, Charles didn't access the meaning of the text and make sure that the understandings he drew from it lined up with the print. Instead, he left the miscue in place and proceeded through the rest of the text without seeing the ways in which he was neglecting aspects of both the print and the meaning.

After reading the biography about Abraham Lincoln, Charles was able to give a superficial summary of the text (that included nothing about bats!). Because Charles understood the gist of the passage, one might argue that getting him to look more closely at the word *elocution* would be of limited value. But a pattern of such inaccuracies could create habits for Charles that are harder to fix than they are to prevent. Furthermore, *elocution* is a very decodable word, made up of chunks that Charles knows, yet he has developed the inefficient habit of substituting known words for unknown words, rather than letting the text help him understand the novel term. Though he manages okay now, this inattentiveness to the details of the print and their connection to the substance of the meaning will likely prove problematic as Charles moves up into grades where the text is increasingly concept dense, is presented in less predictable structures, and includes even more new vocabulary.

Furthermore, by not taking the time to actually decode the word *elocution*, particularly when he was able to discern the meaning of the word, Charles eliminated the opportunity to add this new word to his vocabulary. So, substituting *echolocation* for *elocution* is problematic both because it reinforces an inefficient habit and because it exacts an opportunity cost on his vocabulary development.

Displaying a similar pattern, Ramona, a third grader reading from *Earrings!* by Judith Viorst (1993), read the following passage:

> *They say that I need to be patient.*
> *I've tried being patient.*
> *I'm tired of being patient.* (6)

When Ramona read the text aloud to Jan, she inserted *a* before *patient* on each line. Ramona read as follows:

> *They say that I need to be a patient.*
> *I've tried being a patient.*
> *I'm tired of being a patient.*

Ramona's miscue made sense on a sentence level; she was certainly using meaning! She even justified it on a story level, explaining to Jan that when you get your ears pierced, a doctor uses a needle. With this reading, Ramona wasn't looking closely enough at the print on the page, but rather inserted words that made sense to her. Her insertions, however, completely changed the meaning of the text. Ramona did not work to bring the sense she was making into alignment with what was actually in the text.

●●● Teaching Readers to Align Print with Meaning (and Vice Versa)

Although few miscues (if any) are the result of students absolutely depending on either print or meaning, they are usually the result of students favoring one of these cueing systems over the other. When children don't monitor their reading or engage reading strategies efficiently, teacher instinct often leads us to swoop in with a prompt that will help the reader solve his or her problem. To Charles, we might say something like this:

"Look carefully at that word." (Teacher prompting toward print.)

"Break that word into chunks." (Teacher prompting toward print.)

"Does *echolocation* make sense in this story about Abraham Lincoln?" (Teacher prompting toward meaning.)

"What do you know about Abraham Lincoln?" (Teacher prompting toward meaning.)

Usually, we try to prompt readers to use the source of information—print or meaning—that they are *not* using well. For example, our instinct with Ramona would be to ask one of the following:

"Where is the word *a* in these sentences?"

"Look closely at the print."

"Do your words match the words on the page?"

Ultimately, to eliminate confusion for students, *we* do a lot of digging into the text. However, the practice of using specific prompts systematically overrides students' decision making around *which* strategies to use. Our prompts offer students less and less information that *doesn't* make sense, basically telling them how to solve the problem rather than supporting them in solving the problem themselves. Consequently, students are no better equipped to transfer to new text the strategies we are trying to teach them. Rather than serving as a temporary scaffold, our teaching becomes a permanent support, leaving us to wonder how we can scaffold differently. What if we prompted specifically less often and said, "Try that again" or "What are you going to do?" when students were not aligning print and meaning?

● ● ● Learning to Dance

One of the surprises of Jan's adult years is that she has fallen in love with dancing. From contra, to swing, to waltz, she is an exuberant and clumsy novice. She spends a couple of nights a week absorbed in the "work" of dancing, which is mentally and physically rigorous and ridiculously fun. Much like reading, dancing involves coordinating a host of separate skills and processes. Dancers must remember movements of the feet and the arms, move in time with the music, maintain posture, attend to the mirrored movements and physical cues of their partner, and maintain balance. It doesn't really feel like dancing until you have practiced all these parts long enough for them to become automatic and integrated.

Those who teach dance well not only display a contagious enthusiasm, but also scaffold the beginning dancer in ways that make the complexity of tasks manageable, without assuming the responsibility of the work. The most critical first step (no pun intended!) of learning most dances is mastering the "basic step." Once you learn the basic step, you can begin to try dancing with a partner, integrating arm movements, and even adding your own flair.

The best dance teachers scaffold thoughtfully and flexibly as the student practices the basic step over and over. The teacher may do the footwork right beside you as you follow the pattern, or he or she may do the basic step opposite you, letting the mirrored footsteps support you. The teacher usually counts the steps and gives you simple verbal and physical cues, such as bending when he or she says, "Bend your knees." All the while, you are still practicing the basic step, over and over and over and over. "Now you're getting it," the inspirational dance teacher says with a smile. Regardless of the scaffolding, however, you always do the basic step yourself. Meanwhile, the teacher manages to make you believe that you are coordinated and graceful and born to dance, even as you step on his or her toes.

When you learn to dance, no one moves your feet for you. No matter how much scaffolding you receive, completing the basic step over and over is your responsibility. So the act of simplifying the dance for the beginner can't compromise the integrity of the basic step, because then it would compromise the learning.

In reading, the basic step is the one-two of aligning print and meaning (or vice versa). This integration is the footwork upon which the full reading dance is built. In our opinion, the way we have learned to scaffold readers sometimes interrupts their practice of the basic step. Even more disconcerting, sometimes, we actually do the step for them.

If we can preserve the heart of reading's basic step, however, rather than let our scaffolding do some of the prompting and cross-checking for the reader, then he or she will be stronger in the end. We can do this by letting the text support the readers, and by teaching them to notice what the text is prompting them to do. The *Does That Match?* lesson offers readers a chance to work on their basic step—comparing and contrasting the print and meaning information in the text. Teachers use shared reading to scaffold parts of the text as needed, as the students work to figure out selected words.

• • • The *Does That Match?* Lesson Overview

Does That Match? (Table 3.1) is an exercise that gives students a vocabulary with which to talk about their reading process. It begins by explaining to students that there are two particularly important kinds of work that readers do as they read: decoding the print and making sense of the meaning.

As an illustration of how print and meaning work together, students stand and place their hands on their waist and tilt from side to side. The teacher helps them notice that when they return to standing up straight, the muscles on both sides of their bodies work together, with the muscles on the opposite side of their bodies doing a little extra work to bring them upright. The teacher reminds students that reading requires checking and cross-checking the print and the meaning to make sure they "match," something readers do all the time and do so well that they usually don't even notice it, just like they don't notice the muscles on either side of their bodies working each time they stand up. The teacher tells the students that the lesson they are about to do will help them see the ways in which their reading process works.

The teacher then presents students with a shared reading passage with selected words encrypted using the Wingdings font. Students, with the support of the teacher, use both the meaning and the print to help them think metacognitively about how an integrated reading process works. As they work through the selected text, the teacher helps them notice the way the two types of work—decoding and making sense—support each other. This exercise makes the work of aligning print with meaning, and vice versa, explicit for students. While children may quickly learn the letter-symbol representations for Wingdings, it is important to note that the purpose of this lesson is not to teach children to become proficient in Wingdings! Rather, the purpose is to elevate their understanding of their reading process and to give them a vocabulary for reflecting on it.

Table 3.1

The *Does That Match?* Lesson

PURPOSE	
LONG-RANGE PURPOSES	**IMMEDIATE PURPOSES**
• To teach children to reflect on the ways in which their work affects their learning • To empower children to persist through difficulties	• To help children monitor their reading • To use evidence from the text to support claims about what the text means • To show students that reading miscues are a normal, even important, part of the reading process
STANDARDS	**TIME FRAME**
Reading Anchor Standards: 1, 2, 3, 4, 5, 7, 10 Reading Foundational Standards: 3, 4 Language Anchor Standards: 3, 4, 5	45–60 minutes

MATERIALS
Narrative or informational text excerpt with selected words encrypted using Wingdings font on a PowerPoint slide, chart with icon for decoding work (see Figure 3.1), chart with icon for meaning work (see Figure 3.2), student copy of encrypted text

PROCEDURE AND PRACTICE
1. Begin by explaining to students that there are two special kinds of work that all readers do when they read: decoding the print and making sense of the meaning. Use charts to explain.

continued

2. Ask children to stand and place their hands on their waists and tilt to one side. As they slowly return to the center, ask them to notice how the muscles on both sides of the body work to help them stand up straight. In particular, the muscles on the opposite side of the body have to work a little harder. Repeat using the other side.

3. Write this sentence on the board: *The cowgirl rode her horse.*

4. Next, show students what it looks like when students tilt toward print. Say something like "*If a reader reads this sentence and says, 'The cowgirl rode her house,' we can see how the reader is paying attention to the print because there is only one letter difference between these two words. However, because what the reader says sounds absolutely crazy, this reader needs to think about the meaning and check the print again to make sure they match.*"

5. Then show students a second example. Say something like this: "*If a reader reads the same sentence as, 'The cowboy rode the horse,' what print and/or meaning is the reader using? Do print and meaning match?*" Point out that even though what the reader said makes sense, the reader is not accurately reading the print.

6. Choose a text excerpt and encrypt several words using the Wingdings font. (For detailed text suggestions and recommendations for encrypting, see Appendix B.)

7. Reveal the text sentence by sentence. Depending on the difficulty of the text, either read it aloud or ask students to read the text silently.

8. Using the context and eventually what is revealed about the print, ask students to figure out each encrypted word and explain how they know. For each encrypted word they solve, students should cite evidence from both the print and the meaning.

9. For intermediate grades, distribute a copy of the text with encrypted words. Let students work independently or in pairs to solve the remaining words, gathering print and meaning information to support their solutions.

10. Gather students back together as a group and let them share what they figured out when they worked independently.

continued

11. Wrap up the lesson by supporting students as they summarize the way the reading process integrates print and meaning information.

12. Leave the charts representing meaning and print on display. Tell students to remain aware of the ways they work to make sure that print and meaning match in "regular" text—i.e., text without encrypted words.

Figure 3.1
Chart
Representing
Print Work

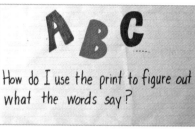

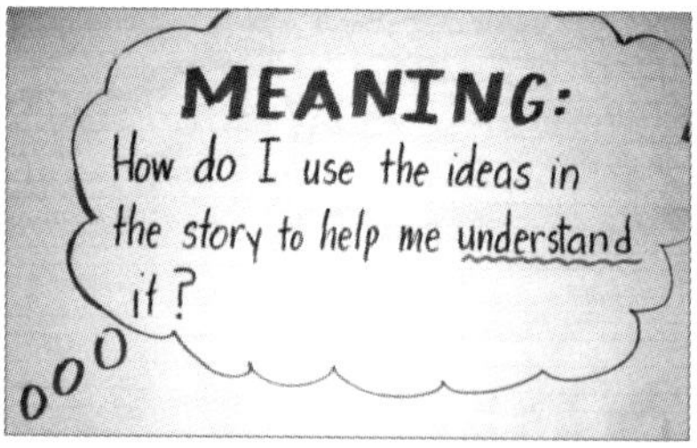

Figure 3.2
Chart
Representing
Meaning Work

● ● ● *Does That Match?* Sample Texts

You can teach a *Does That Match?* lesson with narrative or informational text. When choosing a text, look for something that piques student curiosity enough to make them eager to learn more about the character, problem, or topic highlighted in the excerpt. The text, however, doesn't need to be particularly advanced or complex, because the encryption adds a layer of complexity to the task. Because everyone will be able to see the text as it is revealed sentence by sentence, *Does That Match?* is a shared reading lesson, which allows teachers to adjust scaffolding as necessary. If the text is a little harder, you will read more of it aloud with students following/reading along. If the text is simpler, students will read more of the text around the encrypted words independently. The point is to have students puzzle through the encrypted words. Thus, for the most part, a simpler text can be sufficiently challenging and a difficult text can be made accessible.

In the sections that follow, we offer a sample text with different encryptions, illustrating the way the encryption and the corresponding problem-solving work can vary for different readers. Also, in Appendix B, we include several different texts, including those for beginning readers, with specific suggestions for encryption. As you try this strategy with different text selections, you will begin to notice what makes a particular word more or less suitable for encryption.

The following is an excerpt from Nancy Krulik's *I Hate Rules!* (2003). It features a conversation between two children discussing the previous night's math homework and another child realizing that he has missed this assignment. We chose this text because students relate to it and respond strongly to the character's problem. In addition, it has enough simple words to encrypt for younger readers and enough more-difficult words to encrypt for older readers.

From Katie Kazoo Switcheroo *I Hate Rules!* by Nancy Krulik:

But before the kids could go back to their game, Mrs. Derkman blew her whistle.

"Class 3A," the teacher called out, "let's line up."

"Boy, that math homework was really hard," Katie whispered to Jeremy as they got in line.

"It took a long time," Jeremy agreed.

George looked at them both strangely. "Math homework? We had math homework?"

"You didn't do it?" Katie asked.

George turned red in the face. "I . . . uh . . . I guess I forgot."

"Oh man," Jeremy moaned. "This stinks."

"Why?" Katie asked him. "George forgot his homework. Not you."

"I know," Jeremy agreed. "But George, you were supposed to be in the four-square championship at recess. You're the best four-square player in our whole class."

> *George smiled. "I'm the king. I'm going to destroy the kids in 3B."*
>
> *Jeremy shook his head. "No you're not. You're not even going to be there. You know the rule. If you forget your homework, you have to do it at recess." (6–7)*

The general story line in this text excerpt is relatively easy to follow, but it has an added layer of comprehension work involving the missed recess and the implications for the four-square championship. This extra layer of meaning lends even more substance to the exercise.

••• Sample Text Encryption for Second- and Third-Grade Readers

In the following text, we again present the excerpt from *I Hate Rules!* This time, we encrypt certain words, selected to help readers see the ways in which their reading strategies support aligning the print and the meaning information as they read.

From Katie Kazoo Switcheroo *I Hate Rules!* by Nancy Krulik:

1 But before the kids could go back to their ㄨ☉ℿ, Mrs. Derkman blew her whistle.

2 "Class 3A," the ◆ℿ☉ℿ≈ℿ□ called out, "let's line up."

3 "Boy, that math homework was really hard," Katie ◆≈⊁◆□ℿ□ℿ≙ to Jeremy

4 as they got in line.

5 "It took a long time," Jeremy agreed.

6 George looked at them both strangely. "Math homework? We had math homework?"

7 "You didn't do it?" Katie ☉◆&☉ℿ≙.

8 George turned red in the face. "I . . . uh . . . I guess I ⊁□□ㄨ□◆."

9 "Oh man," Jeremy moaned. "This stinks."

10 *"Why?" Katie asked him. "George forgot his* ⌸○♏◆□□&. *Not you."*

11 *"I know," Jeremy agreed. "But George, you were supposed to be in the*

12 *four-square* ♏⌘○□⊬□■◆⌘⊬□ *at recess. You're the best four-square player in*

13 *our whole class."*

14 *George smiled. "I'm the* &⊬■⌘. *I'm going to destroy the kids in 3B."*

15 *Jeremy shook his* ⌘♏☺⌂. *"No you're not. You're not even going to be there.*

16 *You know the rule. If you* ⚹□□⊬♏◆ *your homework, you have to do it at*

17 □♏♏♏◆◆. *" (6–7)*

All of the words we encrypt in *Does That Match?* lessons for younger readers, such as in the preceding text, are heavily supported by the surrounding context. We are also careful to think about which Wingdings "letters" are revealed with each decoded word, as this gives the readers a cumulative store of print information. We want them to have just enough information to figure out the words with some puzzling. Finally, we choose words for encryption that require readers to look closely at the print while thinking about the meaning, such as *forgot* in line 8 and *forget* in line 16. Students who aren't looking closely or thinking deeply about the meaning will think the two words are the same. When we teach this lesson to second or third graders, we let them work independently after line 10.

• • • Sample Text for Fourth- and Fifth-Grade Readers

Here we present the *I Hate Rules!* text once again, with a more difficult encryption progression. This is an example of the ways we would encrypt this text for fourth or fifth graders. Notice the ways the print and meaning demands increase by varying the encrypted words.

From Katie Kazoo Switcheroo *I Hate Rules!* by Nancy Krulik:

1   *But before the kids could go back to their room, Mrs. Derkman blew her whistle.*

2   *Class 3A," the teacher called out, "let's line up."*

3   *"Boy, that math worksheet was really hard," Katie whispered to*

4   *Jeremy as they got in line. "It took a long time," Jeremy agreed.*

5   *George looked at them both confused.*

6   *"Math worksheet? We had math worksheet?"*

7   *"You didn't do it?" Katie asked.*

8   *George turned red in the face. "I . . . uh . . . I guess I forgot."*

9   *"Oh man," Jeremy moaned. "This stinks."*

10   *Why?" Katie asked him. "George forgot his worksheet. Not you."*

11   *"I know," Jeremy agreed. "But George, you were supposed to be in the*

12   *four-square tournament at recess. You're the best four-square player in*

13   *our whole class."*

14   *George smiled. "I'm the king. I'm going to destroy the kids in 3B."*

15   *Jeremy shook his head. "No you're not. You're not even going to be there. You know*

16   *the rule. If you forget your homework, you have to do it at recess.*

17   (6–7)

For older readers, we encrypt words that have less contextual support, such as *moaned* in line 9 and *destroy* in line 14, and have them begin working independently on line 9. Encrypting these words draws on the more-developed vocabularies of fourth and fifth graders, requiring them to think more deeply about the meaning and look more closely at the print. Once again, we consider the cumulative revelation of the code and the ways in which the context supports the word as we select words to encrypt.

• • • More Ways to Use the *Does That Match?* Process

After teaching students about the ways that decoding and making sense support each other, it is important to help them see how cross-checking can work with words that are *not* encrypted. They need to understand that aligning print and meaning is something readers do with every sentence, even most words, every time they read.

After introducing *Does That Match?* we recommend trying some of the following extensions and variations to help students continue to notice the ways their reading process works. These extensions of the lessons also help establish in the classroom lexicon the phrase "Does that match?," giving you a way to scaffold readers without prompting them to attend specifically to print or meaning. This language, and the concept behind it, can become an integral part of the vocabulary you and your students use to reflect on their reading process, whether they are reading a textbook during a science lesson or reading a comic book under the covers with a flashlight before going to sleep.

Use the language of *Does That Match?* across instructional contexts.

For the *Does That Match?* vernacular and the metacognition it supports to become an integral part of students' reading lives, we suggest asking, "Does that match?" throughout your instructional day.

Use *Does That Match?* during read-aloud.

You can integrate the language and ideas from *Does That Match?* into read-aloud experiences by thinking aloud as you problem solve during the reading. For example, during a read-aloud or shared reading from *Poppy* (Avi 1995), you might think aloud about the word *crouched* in the following sentence and say something like this:

Ooh! Look at this sentence: "One of the two, a deer mouse, crouched cautiously beneath the length of the rotten bark" (2). I'm going to solve this word [pointing to *crouched*] by first looking at the letters while I think about what the story is about. I say the sounds for *cr-* and think about what word makes sense there and starts with *cr-*. I think it might be *crouched*. So, I check the letters in the rest of the word and reread the whole sentence to see if *crouched* makes perfect sense.

In this example, the teacher doesn't make a miscue, but rather illustrates for students the way a reader might problem solve around a word. Such thinking aloud helps students understand the ways cross-checking is an ongoing back-and-forth, and gives them language for reflecting on their own reading process.

Use *Does That Match?* during shared reading.

Using *Does That Match?* during shared reading releases to students even more responsibility for problem finding and solving. Begin by selecting a text that contains several words that students will need to work deliberately to decode and/or understand, such as the following text from *A Land of Big Dreamers: Voices of Courage in America* by Neil Waldman (2011):

> *Rachel Carson's book,* Silent Spring, *shocked Americans by its charges that chemical insecticides were poisoning their nation's water and farmlands. In her study, Carson discovered that traces of DDT, a widely used insecticide, were even present in the breast milk of nursing mothers. By making people aware of the perils of chemical pollution, the book also fostered the beginning of what would eventually become the environmental movement.* (20)

Read aloud from the text as students follow along. As you are reading, stop to let students help you problem solve around words or ideas that are difficult to understand and/or words that present decoding challenges. In either case, students will have to engage print and meaning strategies, using one to confirm the other, to solve the problem.

While reading the text aloud, make some intentional miscues to let students help you self-correct. For example, you might read aloud the word *charges* in the first sentence as "changes." Students will notice your miscue and can then access both print and meaning information that helps them figure out the correct word. As students work to correct the miscue, ask them to describe the print and meaning work they are doing as readers.

You might also highlight a word that you suspect is unfamiliar to students and ask them to use meaning strategies to help you figure it out. For example, from the preceding text, one group of fifth-grade students puzzled through the word *insecticide*. Students noticed *insect-* and deduced that *insecticide* had something to do with insects. They also connected *insecticide* with other words ending in *-ide*, such as *pesticide* and *suicide*, and gathered that it was something bad. Finally, drawing on the context surrounding the word *poisoning*, they concluded that *insecticide* was a poison that was used to kill insects, and that it was actually harming other animals and humans through the water supply.

As illustrated in the previous example with the word *insecticide*, this problem-solving work involves a constant back-and-forth between print and meaning strategies. As students access these strategies, help them notice and label them. Develop two anchor charts, one for recording print-solving strategies, as in Figure 3.3, and one for recording meaning-making strategies, as in Figure 3.4. Students can refer to and add to these charts during reading experiences throughout the day.

Use *Does That Match?* during small-group reading instruction.

During small-group or guided reading, as students are reading instructional-level texts, many of them will notice when their reading doesn't sound right or make sense. They often indicate this by looking at the teacher! Rather than offering a specific prompt such as "Get your mouth ready!" say, "The print and the meaning will match." Or, if students experience confusion, either with the print or the meaning, rather than prompting them to look at a particular source of information by saying, "Does that make sense?" or "Does that sound right?," instead say, "Does that match?" or "Make the print and the meaning match." This places the responsibility for the work on students.

This kind of prompting will not always work, and sometimes you will still need to offer the traditional prompts. Encouraging students to think about the relationship between the print and the meaning, however, will often offer them sufficient support. We do this work with readers of all ages regularly, and the difference in their sense of agency and the ways in which they negotiate the text is profound. Whereas instruction in small groups has historically emphasized one source of information at a time, this kind of prompting compels readers of all ages to integrate their reading strategies, and the results can be powerful. After talking about reading strategies and exploring the ways print and meaning

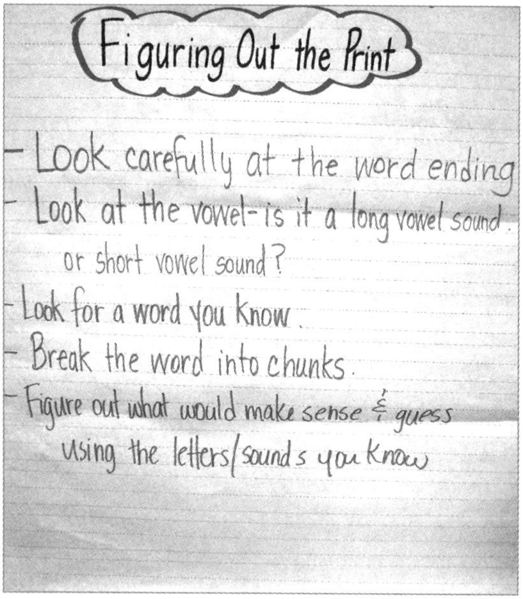

Figuring Out the Print

- Look carefully at the word ending
- Look at the vowel-is it a long vowel sound or short vowel sound?
- Look for a word you know.
- Break the word into chunks.
- Figure out what would make sense & guess using the letters/sounds you know

Figure 3.3
Print Strategies Anchor Chart

Figuring Out the Meaning

- Ask: Does that make sense?
- Reread the sentence slower.
- Reread the sentence carefully.
- Check the title.
- Ask questions and read on. to find evidence
- Make a prediction about what we think and read on.
- Confirm prediction with words from text
- When we don't find evidence, we revise our thinking
- Look back in the sentence before to prove an idea.
- Think about the topic.

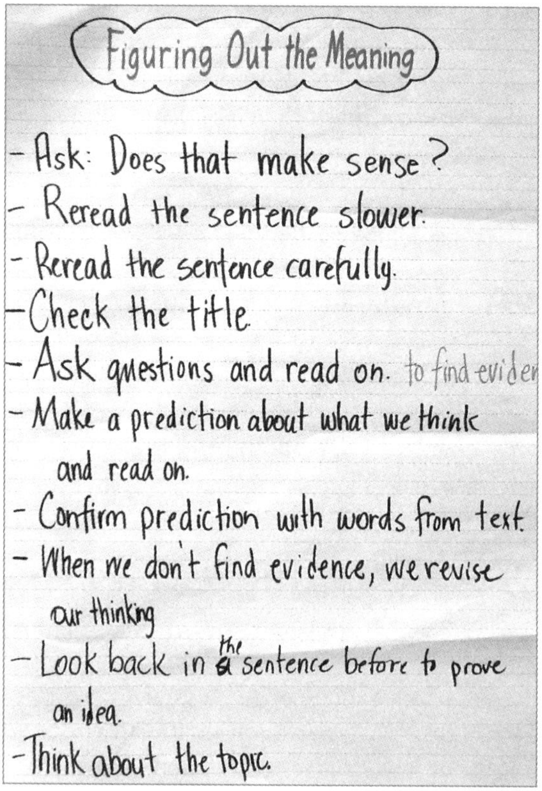

Figure 3.4
Meaning Strategies Anchor Chart

matched in *Henry and Mudge and the Tumbling Trip* (Rylant 2005), Cameron, one of four struggling readers in a guided reading group, announced to Jan, "I'm a really good reader!"

If you create anchor charts during shared reading, you should notice students accessing them during small-group and independent reading. Letting students rely on these anchor charts rather than relying on specific teacher prompts furthers their independence and confidence. The anchor charts should be dynamic tools, to which you can add the strategies guided reading groups naturally discover.

Use *Does That Match?* during independent reading.

After a mini-lesson about asking "Does that match?" invite students to read independently. As they settle in to read, try saying, "Raise your hand when you solve a problem. I want to hear about how you solved it!"

During conferences, let students describe the strategies they use as they integrate print and meaning. Emphasizing alignment in this way, rather than emphasizing specific strategies—such as visualizing or "sounding out"—supports the development of integrated reading processes. Although strategy instruction in isolation is necessary and worthwhile, emphasis on integrated strategies is the ultimate goal, as readers use a combination of many strategies during authentic reading.

For example, Catherine, a third grader, read Jan the following excerpt from *Junie B. Jones and a Little Monkey Business* by Barbara Park (1993).

> *First, I put on my P.J.'s with the feet in them. And then
> my Grampa watched my new front tooth. And he tucked
> me into the big guest bed.* (19)

Catherine said "stucked" instead of "tucked." When Jan asked her, "Does that match?" she went back and reread the text and said, "I said 'stucked' when it's really 'tucked.'" Then she paused and added, "And nobody gets 'stucked' into bed!" In this example, Catherine's strategy work included checking the print, looking closely at the initial letters in the word, rereading for meaning, and considering the structure of the sentence.

• • • Staying True to Our Intentions

In the sections that follow, we consider the ways *Does That Match?* holds true to each of our four intentions: alignment, balance, sustainability, and joy.

Intention 1: We intend toward alignment with our inner teacher.

As we have field-tested and refined this lesson, we have grown to love it! This exuberance follows us into classrooms and tends to make the lessons even better, creating a lovely cycle of energy around *Does That Match?* One aspect of the *Does That Match?* lesson that makes it so endearing for us is that it is, ultimately, about teaching kids to persist when they encounter reading obstacles. While the *Leaning In/Leaning Out* lesson from Chapter 2 supports this kind of persistence in a general sense, *Does That Match?* is specific to reading.

Because the work described in this chapter helps students understand that selecting an appropriate text is more complex than a simple rule for counting words, a whole world of reading possibilities opens for them and shows them that intentional problem-solving work can give them access to words and ideas they once thought were beyond their reach. It is powerful to watch children who previously quit reading after tallying five hard words on a page discover that "too hard" often dissolves with intentional work integrating the print and the meaning information the text offers them. We have found that this realization leads to increased student agency, and is a prerequisite for independence and proficiency in texts, particularly those that are complex!

For example, one group of third graders was working to figure out the encrypted word for sun in the following sentence from *Sleep Like a Tiger* by Mary Logue (2012): "Once there was a little girl who didn't want to go to sleep even though the sun had gone away" (2). Because *sun* was the first encrypted word in the text, the students had very little print information with which to work. They decided with certainty that the word was *day*, but they kept going back to it, monitoring and cross-checking, as they learned more about the story and more about the print. They were relentless, as letter by letter, their supposition fell apart. This relentlessness has become a hallmark of *Does That Match?* lessons, and it is the cornerstone of student success with challenging texts. This tenacity is, for us, the very definition of agency, and the reason we teach. We want children to know that they are powerful, whether they are interacting with text or with the intricacies of their lives.

We find that such persistence has less to do with student reading levels than one might assume. The *Does That Match?* lesson helps readers who struggle discover their power, which is another reason our inner teacher finds these lessons so gratifying. Once, when Kim taught a *Does That Match?* lesson to a group of fourth graders, she used the following excerpt, also from *Sleep Like a Tiger* by Mary Logue (2012), with the words *fine* and *face* encrypted: "Her parents said that was fine. But she should wash her face and brush her teeth" (7). When the students got to the portion of the lesson where they worked independently, Kim circulated around the room, checking in with them to see how they were managing the task. During this time, Kim met Tremalou, a little girl who, as it turns out, was the student in the class who struggled the most with reading.

When Kim pulled up alongside Tremalou, they read the first sentence—which had the word *fine* encrypted—aloud together and Kim supported Tremalou in thinking aloud about the strategies she could use. After conferring with Tremalou for a few minutes, Kim looked at her and said, "You can figure this out now." Then, taking the great instructional leap of releasing responsibility, Kim left Tremalou to work on her own.

At the end of the independent work time, before Kim gathered the students again as a group to talk about what they had figured out, Tremalou approached Kim to show her her paper. Tremalou had figured out every single encrypted word by herself! She hugged Kim long and hard, which brought Kim to tears. Tremalou had not only gained insight into how her reading process worked, but had discovered her power.

Intention 2: We intend toward balance.

Although we said a lot in the previous section about the ways *Does That Match?* aligns with our standards for teaching and learning, the lesson must meet the demands of external standards as well. We find that *Does That Match?* holds up under the scrutiny of the Common Core and other accountability measures. The spirit of the Common Core accentuates teaching an integrated reading process that reaches beyond the traditional focus on isolated reading strategies. *Does*

That Match? requires students to integrate many strategies—using context clues, accessing background information, visualizing, chunking words, and more—as they marry the information they draw from the print and the meaning of the text. This allows students to practice reading in ways that are more authentic than simply reading to practice a single strategy, such as inferring or predicting. Although it is important to teach individual reading strategies, the ultimate goal for all readers is the integration of these strategies.

In one second-grade classroom, the students wanted to insert the word *mom* for *sun* in the line from *Sleep Like a Tiger* that reads, "Once there was a little girl who didn't want to go to sleep even though the sun had gone away" (2). At first, they insisted that because *mom* is a three-letter word, it fit with the code. They went on to use a portion of the meaning, explaining that "sometimes moms go away." After a few minutes of misguided defense of the word, one student piped up and asked, "Then why does it say 'even though'?" His classmates just looked at him quizzically and kept reading. Then another student noticed that the word *the* preceded the encrypted word, which didn't sound "quite right" in the sentence. If the word was *mom*, it seemed to him that the text would say *her* before *mom*. The students eventually puzzled out the word and made sense of the meaning. They did all this without prompting from a teacher. No one pointed out these contradictions to the students or told them when their approximations were right or wrong.

Specifically, if students are going to meet the demands of Common Core anchor standard 10, which requires independence and proficiency in grade-level complex text, they must be willing to notice and wrestle with the ways in which print and meaning interact. In fact, the Foundational Skills of the Common Core Reading Standards are built around this integration, with the third standard addressing word analysis and decoding and the fourth standard dealing specifically with cross-checking. The *Does That Match?* lesson also supports students in meeting the language standards of the Common Core, which require students to use the relationship between context and words to "comprehend more fully when reading."

Furthermore, helping students gain insight into their reading process and providing them with language to consider these processes metacognitively sets them up to tackle new challenges. For example, in an independent reading conference, John, who had participated in a series of *Does That Match?* lessons, talked about encountering the word *Hottentot* in Roald Dahl's *The BFG* (1982, 37). John explained that he didn't know that word on sight, and that he didn't really understand what it meant, either. As for the print, he explained how he looked for chunks he knew, recognizing *Hot-* and *-tot*. Then, he reread to see if he could figure out what the word meant. By going back and thinking more deeply about what he knew about the word *Esquimo*, which had appeared earlier in the text, he was able to figure out that *Hottentot* was the giant's word for "kids who live where it's warm." John's agency and skill, and that of others like him, has shown us the ways this work supports standards-based instruction while also keeping our inner teacher happy.

Intention 3: We intend toward sustainability.

If we had kids attending to their reading challenges all the time with the sort of fervor we just described, perhaps fewer children would have difficulty with reading. Children often read passively, neglecting to notice when print and meaning don't reconcile. Many students also learn to read superficially, particularly as they are assigned hard and/or complex texts. Thus, we, their teachers, tend to take over for them, prompting them in ways that assume much of the work. This response from us, of course, exacerbates the problem, creating in readers more dependency, less self-monitoring, and less agency.

Once students understand that they have many strategies at their disposal, and that these strategies can work together to align the print information with the meaning information, they begin to read like detectives, confident that the solution to their current dilemma exists and that they can find it. After Jan worked with one struggling group of second-grade boys in a guided reading group, helping them develop some metacognitive routines around their reading process, their approach to the text before them changed dramatically. Beforehand, they had hit a plateau in a text that was a Level J. Afterward they dove into a Level L *Horrible Harry* text with gusto and confidence.

Furthermore, the work was theirs. There was no traditional prompting—*Get your mouth ready. Does that sound right? Does that make sense?*—rather, they asked *themselves* these questions and discussed the answers with each other. The work was transformative, for them and for those of us who watched them. We don't imagine that every reader's experience with this metacognitive process will be so dramatic, but we have seen enough powerful responses from students to make us giddy with excitement every time we get to teach a *Does That Match?* lesson.

Intention 4: We intend toward joy.

Although we list joy last in our intentions, it is arguably the most important of the four intentions and certainly the hardest one to meet. Over and over we develop lessons that meet intentions 1–3 but fail when it comes to joy. After we each teach the lesson, we say to each other, "We just haven't met the joy intention yet" or "It fell apart on joy." The lesson may not be awful; it may, in fact, be pretty engaging and very instructionally sound, even good. But that isn't good enough for the joy intention.

This lesson development process can be intense, but we have seen the benefits, so we continue to revise, reteach, and reflect. Such was the seemingly endless work behind the *Does That Match?* lesson. We developed a number of ways to engage students in thinking metacognitively about their reading process, but they weren't begging for more at the end of the lesson. When we looked around the room during the independent work, there wasn't 100 percent absorption in the task.

Finally, we decided to encrypt target words in the Wingdings font. Wow! We were weepy with joy ourselves at the response from students and teachers. We discovered that we could give students the same work we had given them in earlier lessons, and a task previously met with moderate and quickly waning engagement became universally immersive for students. At last, this lesson hit joy in the biggest way possible!

Now when we give students their own copy of an encrypted text, there is always 100 percent engagement in the classroom. Their heads are bent toward their papers, and they are focused. They are determined to figure out what the encrypted words say and mean. From every corner of the classroom, we hear echoes of the same refrain—"I think I figured it out!"—as our work becomes a matter of congratulating them and letting them explain their process to us. Amazingly, children routinely say, "Can we do this again?" as they beg for more opportunities to read text closely and talk about their reading process. The experience is a bit of an instructional nirvana for us. We want to shout, "Booyah!"

Teachers tell us that the *Does That Match?* lesson illuminates for kids what they know. At a time in education when so much public conversation and so many instructional programs focus on and reinforce what students *don't* know, teachers appreciate the energy that rises from work that shows students what they can do. So, although there is abundant joy in the *Does That Match?* lesson, which comes primarily from student fascination with the encrypted words and deciphering the code, we also appreciate the more subtle source of joy: success in the face of a challenge.

••• Closing Thoughts

As readers, children contend with the overlapping sources of information: the print and the meaning. Aligning the work of decoding the print and making sense of the text requires the constant back-and-forth of checking and cross-checking, which involves a host of reading strategies. We can help students become aware of the interaction between print and meaning by engaging them in work that supports them in reflecting on their reading process. As students work to negotiate the text in a *Does That Match?* lesson, they employ connected strategies that demonstrate an integrated reading process. Subsequently, students can take these new understandings to their work in "real" text, where they can continue to reflect on the ways text supports itself. With a strong self-monitoring system in place, reading practice becomes more efficient and productive, which can help move readers along the continuum of independence and proficiency.

••• Questions for Reflection

1. How do you support students in understanding and reflecting on their reading process?

2. How do you support students when they aren't self-monitoring?

3. Analyze your prompts during small-group or guided reading. How well do they develop student independence and agency around problem solving while reading?

4. Where are your day-to-day actions, in and out of school, out of alignment with what you believe is important? What will you do to bring yourself into alignment with your highest ideals?

● ● ● For Further Reading

Preventing Misguided Reading: New Strategies for Guided Reading Teachers by Jan Burkins and Melody Croft (2010)

What Readers Really Do: Teaching the Process of Meaning Making by Dorothy Barnhouse and Vicki Vinton (2012)

Reading with Meaning: Teaching Comprehension in the Primary Grades (2nd ed.) by Debbie Miller (2013)

Stitches: A Handbook on Meaning, Hope, and Repair by Anne Lamott (2013)

First Things First by Stephen R. Covey (1994)

Chapter 4

MINDFULNESS— READING CLOSELY, COMPREHENDING DEEPLY

Wherever you go, there you are.

—JON KABAT-ZINN

You settle onto your three-year-old son's bed to partake in the nightly ritual of reading closely—that is, reading with him in a state of physical closeness. The lights are low. The two of you are intertwined. You are distracted by the dishes you left in the kitchen, but you speak softly of the day, of the book you are to read, of your love for him.

As is often the case, tonight is an exercise in rereading. He has selected the well-worn board book version of *The Carrot Seed* (Krauss 1945), with its chewed corners and its exposed pages where the protective film has begun to separate because of wear. You love the teeth marks on the book as much as you love the familiar story itself. You have read the story many times, and could do so now without even thinking about what you are reading.

You pause before you begin, take a deep breath, take in the smell of your son, the warmth of the bed, the wonder of that moment. And then, for the thousandth time, you begin to read . . . "A little boy planted a carrot seed. . . ."

As you read, your mind walks deep into the story, past the distraction of its simplicity. You think about the boy with the carrot seed and what he is feeling as one by one, all the most important people in his life tell him that the thing he is longing for will not happen. They do not waffle on the matter; they are emphatic. They are certain of his impending failure.

But why? Why do they, one after another, tell him that "it won't come up"? Are they trying to protect him? Are they afraid for him? You flip back and reread. "His mother said, 'I'm afraid it won't come up.'" Ahh, yes. She is afraid, as you often are. You are moved to tears because you understand motherhood's fear. You know the risk of loving, and how moment-to-moment parenting means constantly choosing to be vulnerable. Your son notices your tears. "It's okay, Mommy," he says. He is stronger than you, in many ways, much like the boy in the story, who does not flinch despite his family's lack of faith. You read on as the boy continues watering and weeding and believing, until the glorious moment when the carrot, which had been growing large beneath the earth's surface, finally comes up, "just as he knew it would."

Letting go of your parental fears, if only for this moment, you take another deep breath and embrace the enormity of what your son knows: that everything is going to be okay.

♥ ♥ ♥

In the preceding vignette, close reading takes on two meanings: physical proximity and textual depth. In elementary classrooms, with the ever-rising emphasis on standardized testing, living and working in the moment is challenging, whether reading a bedtime story to a beloved child or teaching a comprehension lesson. These trends and their related pressures are disconcerting for many reasons, but we are most concerned with students' superficial readings of texts, which seem to be on the rise, as readers struggle through texts selected to meet demands for increased complexity. We are not necessarily suggesting that students need to read simpler texts, although this may be the case in many circumstances. Rather, we are saying that whether texts appear simple, such as *The Carrot Seed*, or complex, students need to consistently read "in the moment," giving their full attention to understanding the text.

••• Noticing What Lives in the Woods

In the 1920s, a man named Melville regularly traveled on weekends from New York City to the Catskills, where his family stayed during the summer. While there, Melville took his son, Richard, for walks in the forest to investigate trees, observe birds, and explore nature. This idyllic parent-child communion drew the envious attention of the mothers in the compound, and spurred a trend of father-son walks in the woods.

On Mondays, after the fathers returned to New York City for work, the boys in the compound haunted the Catskills together, talking about and watching the same bird species they had observed with their fathers over the weekends. Once, a boy asked Richard to name a particular species of bird as it flew by. Richard confessed that he did not know the name of the bird.

"It's a brown-throated thrush! Your father doesn't teach you anything!" the boy taunted.

What this boy didn't know, however, was that although Richard's father hadn't taught him to name the brown-throated thrush, he had taught him to pay attention to the bird and notice its behaviors. When Richard and Melville watched the brown-throated thrush, they listened carefully to its song, watched how it flew, and noticed that it pecked at its feathers all the time. What's more, Melville taught his son to ask why, to postulate theories, and to watch even more closely to gather evidence to refute or confirm those theories. So, even though young Richard couldn't *name* the brown-throated thrush, he *knew* the bird because he had paid close attention to it.

In schools, there are many children who read in the same way young Richard's companion watched birds—that is, who do not pay close attention to the text or notice its subtleties. On a recent visit to a fifth-grade classroom, Jan conferred with David as he read *Holes* by Louis Sachar (2000). She asked him to read aloud to her so that she could get a sense of what was happening in the story and how well David managed the print demands of the text. David read the following passage.

> *Stanley dug his shovel into the ground. His hole was*
> *about three and a half feet deep in the center. He*
> *grunted as he pried up some dirt, then flung it off to the*
> *side. The sun was almost directly overhead.* (116)

David handled the words quite ably. He read fluently with no hesitations, so Jan asked him to tell her about the paragraph he had just read. He said, quite matter-of-factly, "He's digging a hole." David could "name" what was happening, but when Jan asked him to tell her more about the text, he couldn't. So they read it again together, sentence by sentence, thinking specifically about the work that Stanley, the main character, was doing in the story. Through reading more "mindfully," David, who had strong background knowledge he hadn't felt the need to access, began to see more deeply into the text. He noticed words such as *grunted* and *pried* as indicators that the ground was really hard. By comparing his height with the depth of the hole, David visualized the size of the hole and considered why measuring it at the center was important. Finally, David thought about the significance of the sun being "directly overhead." David's second summary captured the heat and the heaviness of the work: "Stanley is digging into hard ground during the hottest part of the day. And he's really tired, because the dirt is heavy and he's been working for hours. But he's only about halfway finished."

David's subsequent readings took him much deeper into the text than his first, and his later summary is more closely connected to the main point of the passage. It's important to note that David didn't initially read *Holes* in a superficial manner because he lacked the vocabulary or background knowledge to read it closely. Nor was he disfluent; he didn't have to concentrate on the words so much that he could not direct enough attention to the meaning. Rather, David articulated a rudimentary summary because he wasn't reading wide awake; he wasn't really thinking about the text as he read. David's first reading was like naming the birds in the woods without working to *know* them.

••• Teaching Children to Read Books as Richard Feynman Read Birds

When Melville Feynman took his son, future Nobel Prize–winning physicist Richard, for walks, he didn't teach him the names of brown-throated thrushes and Spencer's warblers, because to Melville, the only thing a name revealed was something about "humans in different places" (Feynman 1988; Gleick

1993). The bird that was a Spencer's warbler in the United States was a *Chutto Lapittida* in Italy and a *Bom da Peida* in Portugal. Melville understood that if you want to really know something, you must pay close attention to it. You must think deeply about it, without distraction.

When Melville read aloud to Richard from *Encyclopedia Britannica*, it wasn't enough to simply "know" that a *Tyrannosaurus rex* was twenty-five feet high and that its head was six feet across. He explained that twenty-five feet was to the second story of their apartment building, and six feet was just shy of the width of their window. With these understandings, Richard could think even more deeply about the *T. rex*, realizing that, although it was as tall as where they sat, it wouldn't be able to get them because its head wouldn't fit through the window! These deep understandings were the result of slowing down, being in the moment of the text, and thinking deeply to unlock layers of understanding.

••• Reading Slowly

Take a breath, dear reader. Seriously. Right now, breathe in and out, slowly. Now take another breath even more slowly. Now notice the way taking a breath centers you, slows you down, brings you into the present moment. What do you notice now that you didn't notice before you took a series of deep breaths? A clock's ticking. A shaft of light coming in the window. The way the wood floor feels on your bare feet.

Your breath is the anchor to being in the moment rather than pulled by distractions; it focuses you. Right now you are reading this book, and with your deep breath you were probably able to refocus your attention on the ideas here and what they mean for you. If taking a breath didn't center your reading, you probably need to pay attention to something more important right now. Perhaps you can close this book and take a walk. We love the idea of you taking a walk.

Rereading is very much like taking a deep breath. Your breath is essential and always with you, just as finding meaning is the essential and ongoing purpose of reading. There is no reading without meaning, just as there is no life without breath. Most of the time, we don't think about our breathing; it just provides the automatic background rhythm for our daily lives. But if we want to do anything better—with more attention and with more care—we can start by thinking about our breathing.

Each breath helps us relax a little more and see a little more clearly, just as slowly reading and rereading helps us understand more deeply. Reading with such focus and intention is a little like slowly walking a path that you regularly rush along, noticing obvious things you've long overlooked. At its heart, real comprehension is an exercise in attention, in doing nothing else. It is about being in the present moment of a text. Integrated comprehension strategies are yoga for the brain, practices that pull us further and further into the moment that is on the other side of the words. We can begin to teach students to better attend to text by teaching them to slow down and breathe.

• • • The *Deep Breathing* Lesson Overview

Deep Breathing lessons offer students a metaphor that helps them read closely. The lesson is designed to help children see the value of reading slowly, rereading, and working to understand the nuances and subtleties of text. The lesson begins with students standing with their hands on their rib cages and taking regular and deep breaths to feel how breathing causes their ribs to rise and fall.

To illustrate how readers' thinking expands with each rereading, just as their rib cages expand with each intentional deep breath, the teacher presents children with an image. The first time the teacher shares the image, he or she displays it for only a moment. On a chart, the teacher records what children gathered from their first "read" of the image. Then the teacher shows students the image a second time, for a bit longer. This time, the teacher instructs the students to notice details that they didn't see during their first read. The teacher adds these details to the chart.

Finally, the image is displayed for the remainder of the discussion. The teacher prompts students to read the image with their deepest breath, noticing details that expand their thinking and finding answers to questions they developed in previous views. As students share these ideas, the teacher adds them to the chart and marvels at how each breath revealed information that expanded their thinking and understanding of the text.

After this demonstration of how to breathe deeply when reading text, the teacher presents students with a second, unrelated text, which may be another image or a short passage. Reminding students to breathe deeply as they read and reread the text, the teacher instructs the children to record all the things they notice and understand about it. Once they have had ample time to read the text closely, the teacher challenges students to a game of *What Do You Know?* in which the students compete against the teacher as they take turns listing details and understandings they gained from closely reading the text. The "team" that accumulates the most understandings wins the game! Table 4.1 includes a complete description of the *Deep Breathing* lesson.

Table 4.1

The *Deep Breathing* Lesson

PURPOSE	
LONG-RANGE PURPOSES	**IMMEDIATE PURPOSE**
◗ To help students learn to think deeply as they read ◗ To show students the value of reading slowly and rereading	◗ To teach students to read complex texts closely by rereading, questioning, and making inferences
STANDARDS	**TIME FRAME**
Reading Anchor Standards: 1, 2, 3, 4, 7, 10 Writing Anchor Standards: 8, 9 Speaking and Listening Anchor Standards: 1	45–60 minutes
MATERIALS	
An image that invites discussion; some way to share the image with students, such as a document camera, projection system, image in poster form, or big book; chart paper; markers in three different colors; a text excerpt	

continued

PROCEDURE AND PRACTICE

1. Ask students to stand and place their hands on their rib cages and breathe normally. Direct them to feel the slight rise and fall of their lungs beneath their fingers

2. Next, ask students to take a deep breath, inhaling for two seconds and exhaling for two seconds. Hold up your hand, raising two fingers to count the two-second inhalation and lowering the same fingers to count the two-second exhalation. Ask students to notice the dramatic difference in the rise and fall of their rib cages in comparison to the first, quick breath.

3. Finally, tell students that you want them to take a deep, deep breath, inhaling for five seconds and exhaling for five seconds. Again, show the count by raising and lowering your fingers. Explain that breathing deeply expands our lungs. When we don't breathe deeply, we don't use all of our lungs.

4. Now tell students that if we take the equivalent of a deep breath as we read, we can expand our thinking about and understanding of a text. The more deeply we breathe in the text, the more understanding we have. We don't get all the information we need from the text when we read quickly.

5. Have students sit down again and explain that you are going to illustrate the difference between a shallow reading breath and a deep reading breath. Begin by displaying an image for only a moment (two seconds or less).

6. Ask students to share what they noticed about the image. Write their observations on a chart.

7. Display the image a second time, leaving it up a bit longer than the first time (three to five seconds). Ask students to notice something that they didn't notice the first time.

8. Ask students to share what they noticed again. Add their new observations to the chart, using a different-colored marker. Point out that their thinking is getting deeper!

9. Before showing students the image the third time, ask them what questions they have about it. What points of confusion do they want to clarify when they look at the image the third time?

continued

10. Display the image a third time and leave it there. Once again, prompt students to notice details that went unnoticed on the first two readings. Ask them to search for the answers to their questions.

11. Add their ideas to the chart in a different color, and comment on how "rereading" or "taking deeper breaths" has expanded their thinking about and understanding of the image.

12. Next, provide students with a text excerpt to read using their deepest breath.

13. Instruct students to notice as much as they can from the text and challenge them to a game of *What Do You Know?*, where the object is to breathe more deeply than the teacher. In this game, the students and the teacher take turns combing through the details and nuances of the text and contributing one additional understanding during each round of play. A player shares his or her understanding by saying, "I know that . . . , because . . . ," citing evidence from the text to support the understanding.

14. The game continues, line by line, until one team (students or teacher) thinks the text has been exhausted and there is not a single thing more to understand about it. The team that contributed the most ideas/understandings wins.

NOTES

- The competition is between the students and the teacher. We do *not* intend for students to compete against each other in this game.

- When introducing the metaphor of breathing deeply to understand the text, some students benefit from practicing with multiple images before moving to traditional text.

- We don't introduce *What Do You Know?* to primary students until they've had many experiences practicing deep breathing with images and shared text. We have found that, particularly when you first teach a *Deep Breathing* lesson, looking at an image three times is often enough of a game for young children.

••• *Deep Breathing* Sample Lessons

The objective of a *Deep Breathing* lesson is to help children recognize the virtues of rereading to discover the nuances of a text. Consequently, it is of utmost importance that you take great care in selecting images and text excerpts that have layers of meaning and subtle details so that students can practice reading deeply—i.e., texts that they will love, for "Love brings us in close, leads us to study the details of things, and asks us to return again and again" (Lehman and Roberts 2014, 2). We do not mean for you to use images with a lot of details for students to simply name and list. Rather, the image needs to have a handful of important details, the noticing of which is essential to understanding the message of the image.

Most important, the purpose of a *Deep Breathing* lesson is to support students in reading text closely to draw inferences. The images in these lessons serve purely as a metaphor for reading traditional texts closely. For *Deep Breathing* lessons, we do not select images that relate to the text in theme or in content, nor are the images intended to build background for later understanding of the text.

Rather, the point of the image work in a *Deep Breathing* lesson is to teach students the process of looking at a "text" three times, gathering new understandings with each reading. Once students are comfortable using the *Deep Reading* process in text, we discontinue the use of images, because the goal is deeper comprehension of written text, not close reading of images. In the sample *Deep Breathing* lessons that follow, we share examples of image-text pairings.

Sample Lesson 1: *Deep Breathing* with Primary Readers

With young readers, we often introduce *Deep Breathing* with an animal image, such as the picture of monkeys shown in Figure 4.1.

When we show this image to students for a quick first read, children inevitably tell us it is a picture of three monkeys. After they have a chance to look at the image a second time, they notice that one monkey is "doing something to" the other monkey and that they are sitting close to each other. With each additional viewing, their thinking becomes increasingly inferential.

They squeal with delight, usually with the third reading, as they notice the baby nestled between the legs of the monkey on the left. They infer that "the big monkey is the mom," that the "two little monkeys are related" and could be "brother and sister, or twins," and that the monkeys are "picking insects off of each other."

We always ask students to explain *how* they know something when they make an observation about the "text." Oftentimes, students discover the ways their background knowledge and the information from the text work together to help them infer. This work supports even the youngest readers in making inferences.

Figure 4.1
Monkey family image for
Deep Breathing lesson

Next, we present students with a print text, such as the following excerpt from "A Storm Is Coming" by Keith Pigdon (2003). This wonderful, informational text from Okapi Educational Materials offers a child's perspective hour by hour as she anticipates an oncoming storm.

> *11 o'clock*
>
> *It is very hot.*
>
> *A strong wind is blowing.*
>
> *The ants on the ground are very busy.*
>
> *I think a storm is coming.* (7)

12 o'clock

It is still very hot.

There are lots of dark clouds in the sky.

A storm is coming. (9)

After reading it aloud the first time, we remove the text from view and ask students to tell us what they understood from their first, quick exposure to it. Invariably, they tell us what they remember from the last sentences: "There are lots of dark clouds" and "A storm is coming."

Then we bring the text back for a second read. This time, as they echo-read the text with us, we remind them to breathe more deeply, and challenge them to discover something that they didn't notice the first time through. After the reading, they share new information from the text, such as "The ants are busy" and "There are dark clouds in the sky." On the third reading of the text, we engage students in choral reading. We remind them to take their deepest breath and expand their thinking. Because they have already recounted all the details, they are tasked with really thinking about the meaning of the text. Here are some of the understandings students typically notice with this text:

- The movement of the ants is a clue that a storm is coming.

- The ants are busy because they want to get somewhere safe before it starts raining.

- The girl in the story knows a lot about storms.

- At 11:00, the girl *thought* a storm was coming. At 12:00, she is sure a storm is coming.

- The dark clouds formed between 11:00 and 12:00.

- It is probably summertime.

- The girl in the text is outside.

- It hasn't started to rain yet, but it's going to very soon!

Students often gather that the girl in this text is following the development of a storm across a day. At the end of the lesson, we share the whole book with students, including the illustrations, which prompts further discussion and confirms many of their assumptions about the text.

Sample Lesson 2: *Deep Breathing* with Intermediate Readers

When we select images for older readers, we often scour picture books for rich illustrations that we can place beneath a document camera. Other times, we select artwork available in the public domain, such as Winslow Homer's intriguing painting *The Gulf Stream*, included as Figure 4.2. In both cases, our objective is to locate images with just enough interesting details to support layers of meaning, inviting multiple interpretations and rich conversation.

With the first glance at this painting, children immediately say it is a picture of a "guy in a boat." When they look again, they start to comment on the approaching storm and choppy waters, and many notice that there are sharks swimming around the boat. As they take their third and deepest breath, they take note of subtler details, such as the broken mast, and they wonder why the man is lying down instead of trying to protect himself. They begin to count the sharks and notice that there aren't just one or two, but rather, the boat is surrounded by sharks. This noticing invariably prompts someone to predict that when the storm hits, it will knock the man from the boat and "the sharks will get him."

Figure 4.2
Winslow Homer, *The Gulf Stream* (1899). Oil on canvas; 71.5 x 124.8 cm. Metropolitan Museum of Art.

Students usually debate the man's chances of survival on a broken boat in the middle of the sea surrounded by sharks until someone less involved in the debate and more involved in looking very closely notices that in the bright white cloud in the upper left of the painting is a faint outline of something that could be a ship. The children squint as they move in to take a closer look, confirming that it is indeed a ship. Many students revise their predictions of doom for the lone sailor and wonder aloud whether there might be hope after all, whereas others argue that the ship is too far away to rescue him.

Depending on the group, *Gulf Stream* provides an opportunity to discuss the civil rights movement. With support from the teacher, the image's metaphorical implications can offer students an opportunity to stretch even further as they "breathe" through the text. *Gulf Stream* can show students the ways in which artists and illustrators use metaphor to make strong statements about complex topics.

Noting how their thinking about this painting has grown with each rereading, we explain that whether reading a painting or reading a written text, it is looking closely and thinking deeply that leads to deeper understandings. We ask students to take a long, deep focusing breath with us as we count to five on our fingers with the inhalation and the exhalation. Then we present students with a short text excerpt, such as this one from Jean Little's *Hey World, Here I Am!* (1986).

> *A long time ago, last August or September, I took a five-dollar bill from Mother's purse. I even forget, now, what I needed it for. She was sleeping and I didn't want to bother her. I think I had to pay a fine at the Library and pick up some shoes that had been repaired. I really don't know.*
>
> *I was going to tell her, though, as soon as I got back, but I forgot. And she never missed it. When I did remember, she was at work. I kept forgetting—and remembering again, always at the wrong time.* (38)

After either reading the text aloud or giving students time to read it independently, depending on the group, we invite them to confer with a partner and reread it with their deepest breath. In preparation for a round of *What Do You Know?*, students engage in conversations with partners or in groups, sharing their literal and inferential understandings of the text. Then they take turns with the teacher adding ideas about the text, including observations such as these from the preceding text excerpt:

- A child in the story took money from his/her mom's purse.

- The child is forgetful.

- The child is a girl/boy. (This always causes an interesting debate as stereotypes inevitably surface. Those on the "girl side" cite paying a library fine and picking up shoes at a repair shop as evidence, and those on the "boy side" cite being forgetful.)

- The child is responsible. (This comment arouses another interesting debate. Some argue that because the narrator took it upon himself/ herself to pay the library fine and pick up the shoes, he/she is responsible, whereas others argue that overdue library books are a sign of irresponsibility.)

- The mother works hard.

- The child lives in the city.

We love this text excerpt for all the layers of meaning students can discover as they read and reread. Inevitably, a lively discussion emerges as students weigh in on whether they think the character's actions were right or wrong. We usually end up sharing with students the remainder of this chapter from *Hey, World, Here I Am!*, giving students even more fodder for discussion.

• • • Picture Books and *Deep Breathing* Lessons

Although we favor pictures and text excerpts for *Deep Breathing* lessons, this strategy also works well with picture books. Select titles that have enough substance to read them three times and discover something new with each reading. Books that have illustrations that carry or extend the story work well, such as those on the following list.

Tough Boris by Mem Fox (1998)

The Giving Tree by Shel Silverstein (1964)

The Wretched Stone by Chris Van Allsburg (1991)

Goodnight, Gorilla! by Peggy Rathman (1996)

Snow Day! by Lester Laminack (2010)

Roller Coaster by Marla Frazee (2006)

The Fantastic Flying Books of Mr. Morris Lessmore by William Joyce (2012)

Leonardo, The Terrible Monster by Mo Willems (2005)

City Dog, Country Frog by Mo Willems (2010)

Silver Packages: An Appalachian Christmas Story by Cynthia Rylant (1997)

Zachary's Ball by Matt Taveres (2000)

• • • Ways to Extend the *Deep Breathing* Lesson

Once you have introduced the *Deep Breathing* metaphor, you can use it to support students as they think deeply about any text. There are also a number of extensions to this lesson, three of which we describe here.

Teach students to take a deep breath before reading.

Although the preceding lesson introduces a deep breathing metaphor for reading closely, you can reinforce the lesson concepts by teaching students to literally take a slow breath before delving into a text. Taking a breath before reading can become a prereading ritual that reminds students of the thinking work for which they are preparing. Initiating reading experiences with a sustained breath offers the physical benefit of calming and centering students, helping them focus on the moment of interaction with a text. This pause before reading also communicates a reverence for experiences with text and invites students to practice mindfulness as they work to construct meaning.

Match generic images with text.

As students become familiar with the *Deep Breathing* metaphor and have had a chance to practice "deep breathing" with images and texts, we sometimes use metaphorical icons as a bridge between the two. We help students extend their thinking by asking them to consider the symbolic meaning of generic images, such as those pictured in Figure 4.3. We talk with children about how the image of a bird pulling a worm out of the earth might represent hunger, discovery, or persistence, while the combination lock could represent protection or maybe problem solving.

After students have had an opportunity to think about the symbolic significance of a variety of images (see Appendix C for reproducible images for this extension), we present them with a text excerpt that is relevant to the curriculum and ask them to think about which image best represents chunks or paragraphs from the text. To respond to this work, children inevitably "breathe deeper" as they reread the text in search of metaphorical connections to the images.

During one fifth-grade social studies lesson, we used the following text from an article titled "An Extraordinary Expedition" from *Cobblestone* magazine (Wilson 2012):

> *The vast country west of the Mississippi River intrigued*
> *Thomas Jefferson. As a man of science, he wanted to*

> *know more about the geography, plants, animals, and*
> *native people who inhabited the area. As a political*
> *leader of the United States, he was interested in the*
> *West as a place for the young nation to expand its*
> *agricultural and trade interests.* (26)

The student discussion around which image best represented this excerpt was rich, with some students arguing that the picture of the lock was the best representation because "Thomas Jefferson was trying to unlock what was west of the Mississippi River." Others insisted that the butterfly net was a better fit because, by studying the West, "Thomas Jefferson was trying to capture his

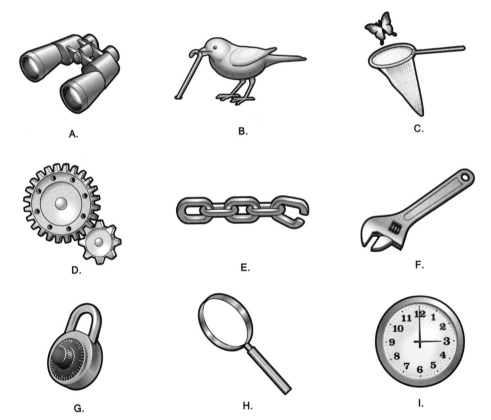

Figure 4.3
Generic Metaphorical Images

dream of expanding the United States." Still others argued that the bird grabbing the worm was the best match, because the excerpt was really about "Thomas Jefferson feeding his curiosity about what lay west of the Mississippi River." In each case, students keyed in to specific details to support their thinking and grew increasingly inferential as they supported their claims with evidence from the text.

• • • Staying True to Our Intentions

As always, evaluating how well lessons meet our four intentions is important to us. Here we consider the ways in which the *Deep Breathing* lesson addresses alignment, balance, sustainability, and joy.

Intention 1: We intend toward alignment with our inner teacher.

Deep Breathing lessons meet the alignment intention because they teach students to read for meaning rather than to read simply to get to the end of the page. For this reason, "breathing deeply" aligns with our goal for students to become lifelong learners, because the practice of taking a deep breath, both literally and metaphorically, when opening a book focuses student attention and paves the way for connections between the text and the reader's experiences.

This transactional relationship was prominent with one group of fourth graders who participated in a *Deep Breathing* lesson with the following excerpt from April Pulley Sayre's *Trout Are Made of Trees* (2008): "Next, the shredders move in: crane flies, caddisflies, shrimp, and stoneflies shred leaves. Rip and snip! They eat the algae-covered leaves, which become a part of them" (12).

Initially, many of these students said that they just didn't "get it." They complained that they didn't understand the words *shredder* and *algae*, and they asked, "What's a caddisfly?" and "What's a stonefly?" Reminding students to take a deep breath and nudging them to see what they *could* figure out prompted them to dig into the text. After rereading several times, one child said, "It says *rip* and *snip* right after *shred*. Shredding must be when you tear things apart." Shortly after that, another student piped up and added, "I know what a shrimp is.

It lives in the water. A crane fly, caddisfly, and stonefly must be things that live in the water, too."

As these students talked through the text line by line, they discovered that they knew far more than they had originally realized. What is more, the students began to excitedly connect what they figured out to a bigger, lingering question they had asked when they first saw the book: "What does 'trout are made from trees' mean?" Gradually, students discovered the overarching message of the book and exclaimed, "Ooh! Ooh! Ooh! I get it! So, like, shrimp and stuff eat the leaves that come from trees and the trout eat the shrimp, so that's why trout are made of trees!" As they marveled at the clever title, we marveled at their ability to access deep understanding with so little support from us.

Intention 2: We intend toward balance.

Although our first priority is keeping our inner teacher content, we cannot neglect the accountability demands on classrooms. Fortunately, *Deep Breathing* lessons can also help students meet the requirements of external standards. In particular, some standards require reading closely and carefully to make logical inferences about text, which is the very purpose of a *Deep Breathing* lesson, as described throughout this chapter.

In addition, even though we teach *Deep Breathing* lessons using fiction texts, they are also particularly helpful with teaching students to read nonfiction closely. It is even common for students, when reading images and texts closely, to make curricular connections to science and social studies. For example, on the third viewing of an image of an ape in a tree from *Animal Feet* (Pyers 2000), students began to notice the ape's fur. They commented on how it was long and "orange-ish." Making a connection to their current science unit on mammals, one boy asserted, "That monkey's a mammal, because it has fur!" Using *Deep Breathing* lessons as an avenue for supporting nonfiction reading not only helps balance student experiences with text types, but also supports student independence and proficiency in different kinds of texts.

Intention 3: We intend toward sustainability.

The work of *Deep Breathing* lessons supports students in developing many sustainable practices. We have described most of these—such as agency, problem-solving strategies, inferential thinking, and deepened comprehension—in previous sections of this chapter. Teaching students the literal practice of breathing deeply, which is new to this chapter, has become an important dimension of our instruction. With a little support, students easily learn to take a moment and a deep breath to focus before they read any text.

This practice has a lovely effect on readers, one we think supports their overall wellness as well as their reading wellness. Taking a deep breath before engaging with a text aligns with what we believe about learning, reading, and even living. It also holds the potential, if habituated, to offer students lifelong support for mindfulness, which ultimately connects to their happiness (Achor 2010). We hope that these initial exercises in searching for meaning in text will support lifelong efforts to search for meaning everywhere. We find that well readers are happy readers, who not only learn more, but whose existence helps mitigate our nebulous feelings about the various standards-based intrusions that press upon us. Contented learning is a healthy canary in classrooms.

Intention 4: We intend toward joy.

Deep Breathing lessons are filled with layers of joy. First, closely reading an image and engaging in the *What Do You Know?* game is inherently engaging, even fun. The joy in this lesson, however, does not come simply from the enticement of images and games, but rather from successfully working through a cognitively challenging task. There is something naturally joyful about uncovering new ideas in a text. With each round of discovery, students are increasingly excited about what they have noticed. The anticipation builds with each viewing or reading, and every student in the class is consistently engaged in the work, even spontaneously offering reflective comments about their learning, such as "Oh, my gosh! I didn't see that!" Students look more and more closely, uncovering new observations with each "reading." These discoveries are initially gratifying and eventually escalate to joyous.

We sometimes worry that students will lose their focus, given the contrast between the simplicity of the lesson structure and the depth of thought the lesson requires. We record their observations with each round of looking or reading, however, and are always amazed that their attention actually increases with each layer of investigation. They don't want to stop, which is, of course, our litmus test for the joy intention. Once a student asked Kim, "Will you come back so that we can do something fun like that again?"

● ● ● Closing Thoughts

Reading closely is an exercise in mindfulness; it is about being in the present moment of the text. Focusing attention on the text requires practice, and you can show students how to use their breath both as a metaphor for close reading and as a tool for centering their attention on the text. Deep understandings of text require intention, which is a step beyond simply figuring out the words and gathering the gist of the passage. This practice of thinking deeply helps us work toward our long-range goals of helping students live their whole lives richly supported by learning from text.

● ● ● Questions for Reflection

1. How deeply do your students read? Is reading thoughtfully becoming a habit? How do you know?

2. Are you and your students breathing during your school day, literally and metaphorically? How can you slow down the pace of your work and take it deeper?

3. How are you communicating that noticing the layers of subtle meaning in a text is important in your classroom? What else can you do to support "mindful" reading?

4. Are you "in the moment" as much as you would like to be? How do you know? If you aren't, how will you change that?

● ● ● For Further Reading

The Art of Slow Reading: Six Time-Honored Practices for Engagement by Thomas Newkirk (2011)

Falling in Love with Close Reading: Lessons for Analyzing Text—and Life by Christopher Lehman and Kate Roberts (2013)

Readers Front and Center: Helping All Students Engage with Complex Texts by Dorothy Barnhouse (2014)

Planting Seeds: Practicing Mindfulness with Children by Thich Nhat Hanh (2011)

On Looking: Eleven Walks with Expert Eyes by Alexandra Horowitz (2013)

Wherever You Go, There You Are by Jon Kabat-Zinn (2005)

Chapter 5

STRENGTH—PRODUCTIVE EFFORT AND BUILDING READING MUSCLE

Promise you'll always remember: You're braver than you believe, and stronger than you seem, and smarter than you think.

—A. A. MILNE (CHRISTOPHER ROBIN TO POOH)

It is the middle of the summer, and you have registered for a one-day workshop titled Helping Students Develop a Flexible Mindset. Your husband, who teaches classes on social marketing, has a class from 9:00 to 10:00 on the morning of the workshop, and you decide to leave your eleven-year-old son alone for the first time during that hour. The night before, you pull the Cheerios from the cabinet, tell him that you will be gone by the time he gets up in the morning, and go over emergency routines. You hug him and say, "I couldn't have left you alone like this just a year ago. You are becoming more and more responsible."

The next morning you and your husband leave him sleeping, and you arrive at the workshop in time to enjoy the lovely pastries and fresh coffee. Once the session begins, you don't even think about your son, because the presenter is engaging and the content is exactly what you needed. An hour or so into the session, however, as the presenter is finishing a read-aloud of a picture book and you are about to begin talking with a partner about the main character's mindset, you get a cryptic text from your son saying something about an emergency. In a panic, you jump up and rush into the hall to call him.

He answers the phone crying hysterically; your heart rises into your throat. "Are you hurt?" you ask.

"No," he answers.

"Do you need to dial 911?"

"No."

You exhale. "What is it, John?" you ask.

Pause. "Milk," he responds.

"Milk?!" you exclaim, beginning to get exasperated. Eventually, you ascertain that he spilled the entire gallon of milk and is distressed about how to clean it up and what to eat for breakfast. He is scared and disappointed in himself, not to mention hungry. He says that you shouldn't have left him alone. You are beginning to question your judgment as well.

You get him to text you a picture of the milk, and after seeing the picture (and wondering how he can manage technology so ably yet cannot manage to feed himself), you decide to push him a bit. You tell him to get a towel from the laundry room to clean up the mess, and to find some breakfast. You tell him that you know he can do it, and that there is no mistake he can make that he won't be able to fix or that will get him in trouble. He wails that he can't do it and that you are unfair. He tells you to call your husband and have him come home from class. You say "No," and as hard as it is for you, you tell him you have to go, and hang up the phone.

You return to the session simultaneously relieved and anxious. You are distracted through the next activity, constantly checking the time on your phone. Almost thirty minutes after your conversation, you are relieved to receive a text from John that reads "I did it!" Then he sends you a picture of his breakfast: a raw hot dog with dry cereal, and a pickle on the side. You smile, breathe, and congratulate him, feeling that you have learned more about mindset from John than you possibly could in the whole day's workshop.

Because the teacher-mom in this vignette was not at home when her son was literally crying over spilled milk, she could only provide him limited support, which proved good for both of them. Mother and son realized that when learners step into opportunities that require productive effort, they grow. Based on this idea of productive effort, Chapter 5 reframes the familiar analogy between exercise and appropriately challenging learning tasks (Boushey and Moser 2014; Burkins and Croft 2010; Maley 2010; Shanahan, Fisher, and Frey 2012; Tovani 2004), offering practical ideas that can support your work as you help students select texts for independent reading.

We begin by describing ways to revise common strategies for helping students self-select texts. Next, we describe an instructional strategy, which compares different text difficulties to different-sized hand weights. Finally, after we offer suggestions for working with students who select books that are way too easy or way too hard, we present the *Lifting Weights* lesson, which offers students a revised process for considering texts as they select books for themselves.

• • • Teaching Students How to Select Texts

In conversations about matching students to texts, there is often an emphasis on how "heavy" a book is. How hard is it? How long is it? What level is it? As we describe in the paragraphs that follow, we consistently encounter students whose implementations of the common strategies designed to help them self-select appropriate texts seem to have gone awry. In response, we've revised the ways we teach children to select texts by teaching them to focus on the ways in which the texts help them grow as readers.

• • • Recasting Problems as Possibilities

Across our careers as educators, we have taught children to evaluate text difficulty by teaching them the "five-finger rule." We have both used this strategy in our classrooms and in our work as consultants, and even with our own children. We are often frustrated, however, by the ways in which a text can too easily pass (or fail) the five-finger test while still offering too much or too little resistance, or weight, for the reader.

On a recent visit to a fourth-grade classroom, Kim conferred with Myra, who had picked up Roald Dahl's *James and the Giant Peach* (1961) and was considering whether it was a good fit for her. Following her teacher's advice to check the book's appropriateness by reading a couple of different pages and counting the number of words that gave her trouble, Myra opened the book and read the following passage, in which we have underlined the words that caused her difficulty.

> *And now the peach had broken out of the garden and was over the edge of the hill, rolling and bouncing down the steep slope at a terrific pace. Faster and faster and faster it went, and the crowds of people who were climbing up the hill suddenly caught sight of this terrible monster <u>plunging</u> down upon them and they screamed and scattered to right and left as it went <u>hurtling</u> by.*
>
> *At the bottom of the hill it charged across the road, knocking over a <u>telegraph</u> pole and flattening two parked automobiles as it went by.*
>
> *Then it rushed madly across about twenty fields, breaking down all the fences and <u>hedges</u> in its path. It went right through the middle of a herd of fine Jersey cows, and then through a flock of sheep, and then through a paddock full of horses, and then through a yard full of pigs, and soon the whole countryside was a seething mass of panic-stricken animals <u>stampeding</u> in all directions.* (Emphasis added, 43)

When she encountered each of the words she didn't know, Myra held up a finger on her right hand. When she had no fingers left to hold up, she set the book on her desk and said, "I can't read this. It's too hard."

Without even trying to figure out the tricky words she encountered, Myra was ready to dismiss *James and the Giant Peach*. Kim brought her back to the word *plunging* and said, "This is where you held up your first finger. I want you to try *something* here and see what you can figure out about this word." Myra looked at *plunging* for a minute, then got her mouth ready, chunked the word, and, after struggling with the /g/ for a moment, read it perfectly. She looked up at Kim and smiled proudly. Myra's switch from a hard to a soft /g/, followed by her satisfied smile, indicated to Kim that *plunging* was probably part of Myra's spoken vocabulary. This supported Kim's hunch that *James and the Giant Peach* was probably an appropriate independent text for Myra. Because our ultimate goal is always to support reading for meaning, Kim reminded Myra to reread the sentence from the beginning and see if it made sense. Again, Myra was responsive and successful.

Kim told Myra that our brains work like muscles and that the way she had put forth effort around *plunging* was like letting her brain lift weights. Kim explained that figuring out the word *plunging* had made Myra's brain stronger, and invited her to put forth effort with the other words that were difficult for her.

Myra continued her problem-solving process, working to align the print and the meaning information in the remaining words—*hurtling, telegraph, hedges, stampeding*—with Kim doing less and less prompting, and more and more celebrating. Not surprisingly, Myra's effort was productive; she was able to work through all of the challenges this passage posed, with very little help from Kim. Afterward, Kim talked to Myra about how strong she was becoming as a reader. She asked Myra if she still thought *James and the Giant Peach* was too hard for her. Myra smiled and said, "No. I can read it."

Over the years, we have had many encounters with students, such as Myra, who skip over the words that are difficult to decode or hard to understand. They decide that a book is too hard if there seem to be too many words that they don't know before they even try to figure the words out. Although "reading on" is sometimes a helpful strategy, it doesn't serve students well when they apply it universally and/or never exert any effort to figure out the word or clarify their confusion. Once students understand that the *types* of problems they encounter as they read—as well as the productive effort they put forth to solve them—improves their ability to face increasingly challenging texts, then many problems become opportunities to get stronger rather than reasons to choose a different book. Recasting decoding or comprehension "problems"—tricky parts—as possibilities can change the work and bring new energy to reading tasks, whether they are shared, guided, or independent.

• • • Reframing "Just Right"

Another strategy that is common in classrooms, and that has long been the centerpiece of our efforts to teach students to self-select texts, is the Goldilocks principle. With this approach, children consider aspects of the text—their interest in the topic, the number of words that present difficulty, how well they understand the text, and their familiarity with the series or author—to help them decide if books are "too hard," "too easy," or "just right." Although we appreciate this strategy, we find that it has some prominent limitations when it comes to guiding students' independent reading choices.

Consider Reginald, a second grader who had selected for independent reading *Lions at Lunchtime* (1998) from the Magic Tree House series by Mary Pope Osborne. In a conference, he explained to Jan that this text was just right for him because he *loved* the Magic Tree House, there were hardly any words he didn't know, and he could comprehend "everything" in the story. Furthermore, he said excitedly, "I'm reading the whole series!"

How could Jan argue that this book wasn't just right for Reginald? She could hardly suppress such exuberance for reading, and wouldn't want to! Although the Magic Tree House books *were* just right for Reginald from many perspectives—helping him love reading, building fluency, developing reading tastes, learning about a series—they were less "right" from another perspective: they didn't require much effort of Reginald. Consequently, *Lions at Lunchtime* was limited for him in terms of building new reading muscle and making him stronger. This conflict between developing a love of reading and engaging students in reading work that requires productive effort illuminates the nebulousness of the term *just right*.

To mediate the conflict we feel about restrictive definitions of *just right*, we have expanded it to include a range of text levels rather than a single, specific text level. We explain to students that reading texts that are relatively comfortable for us—those in which we can align print and understanding with relative ease—helps us build fluency and develop tastes for authors and genres. These texts are one of the best parts about being a reader! These books are undoubtedly just right for us, just as they are for students. We also explain that books that pose a number of challenges are also just right, such as the way *James and the Giant Peach* provided Myra opportunities to figure out words, for example. In this revised paradigm for just-right books, which we describe fully in the remainder of this chapter, students work to meet different needs with different books, much the way adult readers do.

• • • Reading Practice as Lifting Weights

We find that shifting conversations about text selection from talking about text difficulty to considering the different ways particular books are just right for different purposes can help students make better book choices and enjoy independent reading more. Students learn that the growth they experience as readers rests less on how heavy, or hard, the books are and more on a variety of connected variables, including how hard *they* work. This knowledge can help them become more agentive, and better able to find the texts that truly further their development. To help expand student thinking around text selection, we teach them about strength training.

At least two aspects of strength training are analogous to reading practice: weight (the amount lifted) and repetitions (the number of times a weight is lifted). All athletic considerations of weight and repetition hinge on attention to form. In this analogy, *form* represents alignment, or how efficiently a reader aligns the print information and the meaning. Form is the litmus test for the appropriateness of a weight for an athlete, just as the ability to decode the words to read for meaning (alignment) is our measure of a text's appropriateness for a reader.

Increasing weight, which is related to how much productive effort an athlete exerts, builds muscle. Similarly, figuring out tricky words and clarifying misunderstandings makes it easier for readers to take on even bigger challenges in the next text—i.e., to lift heavier and heavier weights. Reading texts that are heavy for *them* makes readers stronger.

Secondly, in strength training, repetition develops muscle tone. Lifting lighter weights allows for more repetitions in a given period of time. Similarly, students can read more pages from books that pose fewer obstacles, increasing reading volume and building fluency.

We want the reader athletes with whom we work to consider weight and repetitions as they maintain form, or alignment between print and meaning. To teach students how to self-select books that support them for different purposes, and in keeping with our aforementioned premise that there is a range of books that are just right for each reader, we talk to them about the different kinds of texts *we* read, comparing the texts to different weights. In this conversation, we divide books into four categories, each representing a different amount of weight and degree of effort. We discuss how each type of text serves us as readers, and how we consider each of these reading weights appropriate, even important, for us.

This conversation supports student evaluations of texts within the range of just right, teaching them to consider the nuances of each text by asking, "How does this text help me become a better reader?"

Three-Pound Texts: Light Effort

In this analogy between weights and text difficulty, lifting a "three-pound" weight generally represents the lightest text that is just right for a particular reader. For Jan and Kim, some of the magazines we read, *Veranda* and *People*, respectively, offer us three-pound reading opportunities. Three-pound reading is just-right reading because we find it relaxing and stressless. This past summer, we both read *Open House* by Elizabeth Berg (2001), which was a three-pound reading experience for us. There was little for us to figure out; the reading was mostly light.

Three-pound books build fluency and help us discover favorite authors and titles. Reginald's reading of the Magic Tree House series, as described earlier, is an example of classroom practice in a three-pound book, which was the lightest just-right weight for Reginald.

Five-Pound Texts: Medium Effort

The second-lightest weight in this analogy represents texts that require a bit of effort from us. Five-pound books introduce some resistance, or difficulty, in terms of decoding the print or understanding the meaning, requiring the reader to pay increased attention to form. The reader can still solve most, even all, of the print or meaning problems that arise.

Examples of five-pound texts for us include books such as *A Whole New Mind* (2006) by Daniel Pink and *Imagine* (2012) by Jonah Lehrer. These texts combine science and story to challenge some popularly held beliefs, which creates some dissonance for us. We can, however, work through this dissonance with a bit of intentional effort. Five-pound texts begin to build muscle and continue to develop fluency while still maintaining form. These texts also provide continued opportunities to discover authors, genres, and titles we love.

Morty, a fifth grader Kim recently met, decided that J. K. Rowling's *Harry Potter and the Sorcerer's Stone* (1999) was a five-pound text for him. He said that in terms of print difficulties, certain names such as Hermione and Hagrid caused him to pause, and that in terms of comprehension, he sometimes had trouble keeping track of who was whom. Because he had seen the movie, however, he was able to call on his background knowledge to solve these problems with relative ease. In addition, he told Kim that he *loved* Harry Potter and that he couldn't wait to finish the book so he could read the next one in the series.

Eight-Pound Texts: Big Effort

Considerably heavier than the first two text weights, an eight-pound text presents readers with more resistance than a five-pound text, requiring even more attention to form, or alignment. An eight-pound text doesn't require as much concentrated effort as a ten-pound text, but the decoding and understanding problems we encounter are harder to solve, although we can still solve most of them. Last year, Jan and Kim read Steven Johnson's *Where Good Ideas Come From: The Natural History of Innovation* (2010). With its connections to geography, history, and anthropology, Johnson's book was an eight-pound read for us, requiring us to exert a lot of effort to really understand it.

Because they require more effort, eight-pound books contribute much to making readers stronger, honing problem-solving skills and expanding vocabulary. These books also offer some continued opportunities for fluency development, although these opportunities may be interrupted frequently as the reader stops to address gaps in background knowledge. Because eight-pound reading is generally slower and more difficult, the joy of the reading work tends to come less from the content and more from the satisfaction of figuring out the challenges of the text and discovering our power as readers.

Myra's reading of *James and the Giant Peach*, described earlier in this chapter, is an illustration of a student interaction with an eight-pound book. There were a number of problems for Myra to solve in the text, but she solved them all, even though they required a bit of persistence. Myra's increased sense of agency is a lovely hallmark of eight-pound reading.

Ten-Pound Texts: Maximum Effort

Reading a ten-pound text requires ultimate focus and effort. In spite of the intensity, however, the work is still quite productive. Although difficult, reading these texts introduces us to new vocabulary and/or complex ideas that require additional time to carefully process. Very often, we can read text in this category only for short periods of time before our form starts to suffer. We also read more slowly, and often have to reread to maintain understanding, which means that we read relatively little compared with the volume we can read from lighter texts in the same amount of time.

As we have studied and analyzed the Common Core State Standards (2010) and the research upon which they are based, we have read numerous research studies, many of which were quite complicated. Such studies are ten-pound texts for us. We read some passages many times and discussed them, to make sure we understood them well. Even then, there were portions of some of these texts that we didn't completely understand. We worked to resolve most points of confusion but chose to leave a few gaps in our understanding unaddressed, because it was impractical, inefficient, and—most important— unnecessary for us to work through them exhaustively. Our readings of dense summaries of research, such as *Theoretical Models and Processes of Reading* (Alverman, Unrau, and Ruddell 2004), are similar. Such heavy texts are just right for us because they teach us so much, and because they build our reading muscles, but we can't read them for long periods without needing a break.

Recently, Jan watched Juan, a fourth-grade student, fight his way through a very dense informational text about soccer. As a soccer lover, he was highly motivated. When Jan conferred with him, she was initially skeptical about the text's appropriateness for him, but she watched and listened as he read. Because he had tremendous background knowledge about soccer, he was able to solve many of the problems he encountered, including deciphering the complicated spellings of the names of some of his favorite professional soccer players. However, he simply could not manage many of the print and meaning demands of the text; his form was shaky in many places as he read. Nonetheless, this text was just right for him in many ways. As a complement to the other text weights, there is a place for these ten-pound weights in students' reading lives.

Oddly enough, we have found that teaching students to evaluate texts using four just-right text weights is actually easier, in many ways, than teaching them to identify a single just-right text. Students quickly develop a sense of how their reading process is supported by particular texts. Of course, the categories defined by the weights are qualitative. The point is not to categorize books by weight for its own sake; rather, the purpose is to help students see the ways their individual development as readers can be supported by a variety of texts.

Our labeling of the varying text difficulties as three-, five-, eight-, and ten-pound weights is very intentional. In field-testing this strategy, we have tried different labels, but these incremental numeric weights best serve ongoing classroom conversations. Terms such as *biggest weight* and *smallest weight* become confusing and vague, and we completely reject certain labels such as *heaviest weight* or *level one weight*, because they invite competition. We understand, for example, that in reality, every student's lightest-weight text is relative to that individual reader's needs, even though everyone in the classroom refers to his or her lightest weight as three pounds. We understand that we are bending the metaphor. For some reason, however, using a set of common weight references to identify and discuss the needs of individual readers seems to diminish student competition while also deepening the ways students think about the texts they are selecting.

In summary, the relationship among these four text weights is represented in Figures 5.1 and 5.2. Figure 5.1 shows the way a reader will read less volume—i.e., lift the weight fewer times—with a heavier text. In addition, the Text Weight Guide in Figure 5.2 explains the ways texts of each weight

Figure 5.1
The Relationship
Between Text Weight
and Fluency

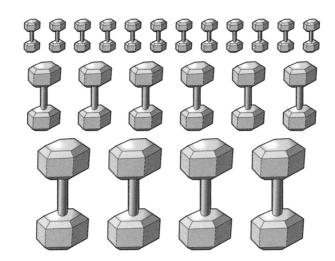

Figure 5.2
Text Weight Guide

Light Effort

Best for developing fluency; least beneficial for acquiring new vocabulary.
Fastest rate; highest reading volume in a given block of time.
Relaxing; involves least effort, and all of it is productive.
There are a very few things to figure out about the print and/or the meaning, but the reader can handle all of them pretty easily with near perfect form.

Medium Effort

Develops fluency and potentially some vocabulary.
Slower rate, but the reader can still read much in a given block of time.
Mostly relaxing; involves more effort, but is still very productive.
There are some things to figure out about the print and/or the meaning, but all of them, with maybe a few exceptions, the reader can still handle independently while maintaining form.

Big Effort

Contributes less to fluency development but much more to vocabulary growth.
Slowed rate; reader reads even less in a given block of time.
Involves more focused effort, but it is still very productive.
There are many more things to figure out about the print and about the meaning, but all of them, with maybe a few exceptions, the reader can handle independently without compromising form beyond recovery.

Maximum Effort

Contributes minimally to fluency, if at all, but can contribute substantially to vocabulary growth.
Slowest rate, as reader must mostly read slowly and often reread; reader can't read for very long without fatiguing.
Manageable stress; involves extensive effort, some of which may not be productive.
There are even more things to figure out about the print and about the meaning, many of which are complex, sometimes disrupting form. Some textual challenges are beyond the reach of the reader without the support of other sources of information.

contribute to readers' development. Both of these images are included as full-page reproducibles in Appendix D.

• • • Books That Are "Too Hard" or "Too Easy"

As much as possible, we minimize conversations about books that are "too hard" and "too easy." Although these terms have long served us and we have been grateful for the ways they have helped us help students, our thinking has evolved in response to student reactions to their connotations.

Books That Are "Too Hard"

We find that telling students that books are too hard for them can be a little like telling a child that he or she is not old enough to watch a certain television show or drink a caffeinated soft drink; our words actually make the ill-fitting book/ show/beverage *more* appealing. Furthermore, we want to congratulate students for work that is challenging or "hard." In so doing, we make *hard* something to long for, which sends mixed messages about difficult books. If reading something *hard* is good, then reading something "too hard" must be really good!

Consequently, we choose to reserve the term *too hard* for books that are truly beyond the reach of the reader, such as a first grader trying to read *Adventures of Huckleberry Finn* (Twain 1885). These text extremes are usually simple for teachers and students to identify, and require little, if any, discussion.

Sometimes, however, it seems that student reading selections teeter on the fine line between a hard text—such as a ten-pound text—and a *too-hard* text. When Kim was a fifth-grade teacher, she had a student in her class, Andrew, who surprisingly selected the unabridged version of *Little Women* (Alcott 1947) for independent reading. Although the text seemed an unlikely choice for Andrew, and Kim was puzzled by his interest, he tackled the book with intention. During each daily thirty-minute reading period, Andrew's reading was slow and methodical. He worked intently to get to know and understand the lives of Meg, Amy, Beth, and Jo. Andrew was really reading *Little Women*, not just pretending to read, but his reading was so slow and intense that after six weeks, he had read only about a quarter of the book.

The effort that it took for Andrew to read *Little Women* was excessive, and compromised the balance of his reading practice. Although the book was really hard and was not one he could read efficiently, it wasn't necessarily *too* hard for Andrew. If Kim had had the analogy of texts as weights, she would have been able to show Andrew how the heft of *Little Women* was more like a fifteen- or twenty-pound weight for him, which made his independent reading practice counterproductive. Then, she could have helped Andrew understand the ways in which other titles would make him stronger, a conversation to which most students are open.

Books That Are "Too Easy"

Books that are truly "too easy" are also obvious, such as a proficient fourth grader selecting the equivalent of *Dick and Jane*. These "too-easy" texts are silly to even consider, and they get less and less attention in our discussions with students. Once again, the labels *too easy* and *too hard* get in the way. Like the term *hard*, the word *easy* can carry negative connotations in the classroom. We find that these nuances, once again, interfere with productive conversations about growing as a reader. Shifting conversations to discussions of effort as the counterpoint to ease and eliminating the adverb *too* help to focus students on their reading efforts as a whole.

Consider Dawn, an able third-grade reader who discovered Mo Willem's Elephant and Piggie series. These texts are written for very beginning readers, but they are funny and always offer something to think about. We would not stop Dawn from reading about Elephant and Piggie or tell her that these books were too easy for her. Rather, we would relish the characters with her and laugh with her about some of their antics. Knowing that she would quickly exhaust Elephant and Piggie, we would then explore with Dawn the ways the *other* books she was reading, books that are five- and eight-pound texts, were supporting her growth as a reader.

We find that as students become interested in optimizing their independent reading, they don't *want* to read books that don't make them stronger readers, whether those texts are overwhelmingly difficult or ridiculously simple. When they *do* choose to read books that are absolute extremes in terms of ease or difficulty, they often have a reason for doing so, and we try to read between the lines (so to speak) and help them consider which *other* texts to integrate into their independent reading to support their growth.

• • • Independence and Proficiency and the Gradual Release of Responsibility

Before we share the *Lifting Weights* lesson with you, we want to address a common question about the four text weights. Teachers often connect these four text difficulties to the gradual release of responsibility, suggesting that the varying weights seem to represent the four instructional contexts common in classrooms: read-aloud, shared reading, guided reading, and independent reading.

Although texts, by definition, increase in difficulty as teachers work across these instructional contexts that form the gradual release of responsibility, the four text levels that we explore in *this* chapter are all within the scope of an individual reader's ability to manage independently. All of these weights fall within the last rung of the gradual release ladder, which is independence.

This range of independent practice is important, because previously, the independent practice we asked of students rarely mirrored the work we did with them in other steps along the gradual release (Burkins and Croft 2010). If students' independent reading does not align to their work with text during read-aloud, shared reading, and guided reading, then we aren't actually following through with the last step of the gradual release. This often interferes with students' development of agency, and it limits what we can learn about their ability to engage in productive effort on their own.

Although our interest in broadening the range of texts students read independently predates the Common Core State Standards, the call for students to become "independent and proficient in grade-level appropriate complex texts" (CCSS 2010) has helped us refine our thinking. Since the word *independent* is in the standard, independent reading practice seems to us an obvious essential.

• • • The *Lifting Weights* Lesson Overview

The *Lifting Weights* lesson starts by engaging students in lifting a series of four imaginary weights, working from the lightest to the heaviest and noticing the ways the work changes with each increase in weight. The teacher introduces the term *effort*, and speaks to the ways effort relates to developing strength. Next, the teacher shows students pictures of weight lifters and engages students in a conversation that addresses the ways weight and effort are related.

Then, the teacher shows students four texts (one for each of the different weights) that he or she has read, describing the ways each text weight poses different demands for reading it well—i.e., reading the print accurately and fully comprehending the meaning. As the teacher describes each reading experience, he or she works with students to create an age- and/or grade-appropriate version of the Text Weight Guide (Figure 5.2), which remains hanging in the classroom as a reference.

Finally, students read independently from multiple self-selected texts and categorize the texts using the Text Weight Guide they created earlier. As students read, the teacher circulates and confers with them. At the end of independent reading, students share their discoveries about the texts they read. In closing discussions, students reflect individually on the ways their text choices helped them grow as readers and whether more reading of the same weight will make them even stronger. A complete description of the *Lifting Weights* lesson is in Table 5.1.

Table 5.1

The *Lifting Weights* Lesson

PURPOSE	
LONG-RANGE PURPOSES	**IMMEDIATE PURPOSES**
• To help students understand the correlation between productive effort and getting better at something • To show students the ways proficient readers read a variety of texts for different purposes	• To help readers select texts that meet their different needs • To help students figure out how to resolve the difficulties they encounter in texts as they work to read the print accurately and to fully comprehend the text's meaning
STANDARDS	**TIME FRAME**
Reading Anchor Standard: 10 Speaking and Listening Anchor Standards: 1, 2, 4	45–60 minutes

MATERIALS
Two pictures of bodybuilders lifting hand weights (a woman lifting a very heavy hand weight and a man lifting a visibly lighter hand weight) for displaying permanently in the classroom; chart paper and markers; at least four examples of text: one that fits each weight category for the teacher demonstrating the lesson

PROCEDURE AND PRACTICE
1. Ask students to stand up and get ready to work out. Have them imagine picking up a three-pound hand weight as you pretend to do the same. Ask students to join you doing bicep curls with this weight. Describe their efforts, noting that lifting the three-pound weight is quite easy. Point out that this weight lets them do several repetitions for a long period of time while keeping their backs straight and their elbows by their sides.

continued

2. Continue lifting each of the other three weights with students: five-, eight-, and finally, ten-pound hand weights. As students work through this progression of imaginary weights, comment on how each increase in weight requires a little more effort. As the imaginary weights get heavier and heavier, students will slow their repetitions as they pretend to exert more effort, find it more difficult to maintain form, and tire more quickly.

3. Ask students to return to their seats. Show students the pictures of the male and female athletes lifting weights, and ask them to think about how lighter and heavier weights contribute to a workout. Explain that even when athletes *could* lift heavier weights, they often choose to spend some time lifting lighter weights because they can lift the lighter ones "more times." The lighter weights give their muscles tone, whereas the heavier weights make their muscles bigger.

4. Explain that in the same way that athletes vary their exercise by using lighter *and* heavier weights, depending on whether they want to tone or grow muscle, readers vary their text selections to help them get better in different ways. When readers want to practice making their reading sound smooth and expressive, they can work out with a lighter book, or a text that is easier for them. When they want to grow new reading muscle, they can work in heavier, or more difficult, books and practice working through the tricky parts to understand what they are reading.

5. Show students examples of each of the four different types of reading represented on the Text Weight Guide by sharing texts from your own reading life. Pantomime lifting the corresponding weight for each text. In other words, as you share the easiest text, lift as you did with your earlier, imaginary demonstration of lifting three-pound weights. As you share each text, explain the qualities that help you decide whether a book is a three-, five-, eight-, or ten-pound text for you. Also, talk about the ways your reading varies with each text, considering productive effort, fluency, rate, stamina, and form.

6. On chart paper, create an age- and/or grade-appropriate version of the Text Weight Guide (Figure 5.2), recording the points mentioned in your explanations and during conversations with students.

continued

7. Give students time to read independently. Before they begin reading, ask them to think about the productive effort required to read a particular text. Ask them to use the text weight chart you created together to help them categorize the weight of their books.

8. At the end of independent reading, gather students together again. Pose the question "How did your text help you become a better reader?" Ask students to share their responses with a partner, a small group, or the whole class.

NOTES

- It is critical that you communicate the specific, designated value of all four weights—for example, three pounds, five pounds, and so on—regardless of a reader's reading level, because one of the purposes of the lesson is to minimize student competition around book length and size.

- Using an image of a woman lifting heavier weights alongside an image of a man lifting visibly lighter weights helps us counter gender stereotypes that naturally arise during conversations about physical strength.

- It can be helpful to bring in an additional book that is very thick but is still a three-pound weight for you. This helps students understand that the weights are metaphors and have nothing to do with the size or weight of the actual books.

- Your language choices in reference to the weights are critical. Avoid calling the graduated weights "levels," as students are quick to mistakenly assume that the "heavier" the text, the better the text selection. Instead, emphasize productive effort. For example, a student reading a below-grade-level text—an eight- to ten-pound weight for that student—can work harder and engage in more productive effort than a student reading an above-grade-level text, which is a three- to five-pound weight for that student.

••• *Lifting Weights* Sample Lessons

The primary purpose of the *Lifting Weights* lesson is to support students' independent interactions with texts as they engage in productive effort and reflect on their work. For this reason, this lesson provides time for students to read independently as teachers confer with students. The sample lessons that follow are not variations on the introductory lesson in Table 5.1, but rather are examples of additional lessons that can refine student skill as they learn to select different texts to support their different kinds of growth.

Sample Lesson 1: Pack Your Bags!

Objective

To help children develop their understanding of how different text weights serve different purposes for readers.

Preparation

You will need an empty backpack. Gather a selection of texts that represent a cross section of the different kinds of reading you do on a day-to-day basis. For example, you might select a few texts from among the following: a magazine, a newspaper, a research article, a manual for a piece of technology, a cookbook, a travel guide for your destination, a light novel, a complex novel, a textbook, and a nonfiction text about a topic of interest. Make sure to include at least one text that represents each of the weights on the Text Weight Guide (Figure 5.2).

Procedure

Explain to students that you are preparing for a really long flight and are choosing which texts you will take in your backpack to read during the airplane ride. Think aloud about each of the texts you brought as you consider its relative "weight" or what that text offers and requires of you as a reader. Describe for students the purpose that each text serves in your reading life. After describing each text, make a final selection of three texts to place into your backpack. Make sure the three texts represent different weights for you, providing a complement of reading opportunities.

Sample Language

"Of course, the first thing I'm going to pack is this new novel by my favorite author! Because she writes really interesting mysteries, I have to pay close attention to make sure I don't miss anything, which makes most of her books five-pound weights for me. Though I am so excited about this book that I could probably read it during the entire flight, I also have some other reading I need to do. I'm taking a graduate course and I have to read this article. It's a ten-pound weight for me. Because it's really hard, I will work on understanding the article until it wears me out, and then I'll read something more relaxing. Finally, I am going to throw in this magazine. Most of it is a three-pound weight for me, so I can read that when I get tired."

Independent Work

Ask students to consider their own reading lives and the different kinds of reading they do. Ask them to pretend they are taking a trip and to select at least three texts to pack for their own imaginary airplane rides.

Closing

Gather students and have them share, with partners or in small groups, the three texts they chose and explain their reasons for each selection. As students are sharing, circulate and listen to their explanations, noting who seems to understand the varying text weights and who needs more support.

Sample Lesson 2: Lifting Well

Objective

To help students understand that working out at maximum effort causes fatigue, which can compromise a reader's reading process

Procedure

Explain to students that although you have three-, five-, and eight-pound weights at home, you have decided that from now on, you want to use only your ten-pound weight in your workout. Pantomime the process of lifting the ten-pound weight several times, demonstrating increasing fatigue and noticing aloud when the exertion causes you to compromise your form. Connect the weight-lifting analogy to reading heavy texts. Tell students that the athlete's form is like a reader's reading process: everything needs to align as much as possible (see Chapter 3 for more information about alignment).

Sample Language

"Watch me work out with this ten-pound weight! Since this is the heaviest weight I can lift well, it is the weight that will help me build the most muscle. I want as much muscle as I can get, so I've decided not to lift any other weights." (Lift the imaginary weight slowly, exhibiting modest strain.)

"As I'm lifting, I'm focusing on the work my arm muscle is doing. I stand up straight and bend my knees, lining up my body so that my arm does all of the work. The way my whole body works together to help me make my arms stronger is called my form. If my form is good, then I am lifting well. So, I want to hold my legs, elbows, and back just right so that they don't do the work instead of my arms. Boy, my form is looking good right now. See how everything is in alignment? I can really feel my arm muscle working harder and harder. I'm lifting this heavy weight well right now."

(After a few repetitions, demonstrate that the work is getting really hard.) "Phew. My arm muscle is really starting to hurt. Uh-oh! Did you see that? My elbow just moved from side to side. I'm finding it harder to keep my back straight as I get more tired and this weight feels heavier. Uh-oh, now I feel my back is doing more and more of the work, not my arm. This is not good! My body isn't lined up right anymore, so I'm not lifting so well. My arm muscle isn't going to get stronger if my back is doing the work, and I could really hurt my back this way. This wasn't happening when I first started my workout, but now I'm getting really tired, so my form is getting worse and worse."

(Set down the weight.) "I don't think I can lift ten pounds well all the time, as I thought I could. But I don't want to stop exercising. I know: I can switch to a lighter weight, keep lifting, and get my form back into alignment so that my arms do the work." (Pantomime lifting a lighter weight a few times with correct form.)

"Just like we don't want to always lift the heaviest weights in a workout because it is hard to lift them well for a long time, we don't want to always read the books that are the very hardest books for us. Reading only hard, hard books would make us too tired, and our reading process, which is like our form when we exercise, would get out of alignment and we would stop reading *well*. For example, we might start skipping words we don't know instead of trying to figure them out. Or we might not really understand parts of the text but keep on reading anyway.

"If you read for a long time with your reading process out of alignment, you can really hurt your ability to read well, just as you could hurt your back if you lifted really heavy weights without good form. You could get into the habit of not trying to read for meaning and you could even start skipping over the tricky parts as you read instead of trying to figure them out! That would be terrible! Imagine what would happen to your reading muscles if you stopped solving problems.

"So it's really important to pay attention to how well we are reading. Ask yourself, are you figuring out the words and the meaning in the books you are reading, no matter how heavy they are? If not, you might want a lighter weight."

Independent Work

As students shift to independent reading, ask them to spend some time in at least two books that are different weights for them. Tell them to notice their form, or how *well* they are reading, and the ways their reading changes as they read heavier texts.

Closing

Gather students together and let them share the ways text weight influenced their reading process, or form. Reinforce the idea that readers can lift heavy texts only for as long as they can read them well—i.e., read for meaning.

• • • What *Does Lifting Weights* Look Like During Independent Reading?

Because the introductory and sample lessons in this chapter are extensive in their own right, we don't include extensions for the *Lifting Weights* lesson. After reading the first half of this chapter and the subsequent lessons, however, you probably have questions about the practicalities of managing student's independent reading when the term *just right* refers to several different texts. You may need to adjust your classroom routines around text selection, library checkout, reading logs, and more if you are reframing "just right" for your students.

Fortunately, there are lots of ways to do this work well, and it does not have to be complicated. Calling students' attention to the ways they can round out their independent reading does not need to involve mathematical calculations, complicated grids, or dividing forty minutes of independent reading into separate blocks of time for each text weight. We want students to beg for more time to read the books they select for themselves, and efforts to micromanage their encounters with texts of different weights will violate the very spirit of independent reading, the idea of which makes our inner teacher want to cry! So when you think about the distribution of student attention to different text weights, stay true to the spirit of recreational reading while still nudging its boundaries.

There are many ways for students to vary the weight they lift during independent reading. The scenarios that follow offer a few examples of the ways students can broaden their independent reading to include some self-directed, productive effort without stifling the relaxed atmosphere that is the hallmark of independent reading. As you will notice, we don't expect students to read from all four text weights at once. Most of the time, students are reading from two weights, and sometimes three. Here are a few examples of the ways students might vary text difficulties as they read independently:

- Quinton, a fifth grader, finds that some portions of Rick Riordan's *The Lost Hero* (2010) are more difficult than others. This one text gives him both five- and eight-pound reading practice, and sometimes even ten-pound practice.

- LaShanda, a second grader, is reading *Dinosaurs Before Dark* (1992) by Mary Pope Osborne. During roughly the first twenty minutes of independent reading time, she breezes through four chapters of this book, which is a three-pound text for her. LaShanda spends the remaining time reading *Dinosaurs* (Osborne and Osborne 2000), the Magic Tree House research guide, which is the nonfiction companion to *Dinosaurs Before Dark*. This book gives her eight-pound reading practice while also extending her understanding of *Dinosaurs Before Dark*.

- Steven, a fourth grader, is captivated by *The American Boy's Handy Book: What to Do and How to Do It* (Beard 2008). This book is filled with procedural text and includes information about irresistible topics, such as how to build your own boat and how to camp out without a tent. The text, however, was first published in 1890, which means it has some pretty sophisticated language, making it a ten-pound read for Steven. He has to read each passage several times to understand it. Steven begins his workout with this text, stopping when he grows fatigued, which is usually after about ten to fifteen minutes. Then, Steven switches to *Diary of a Wimpy Kid* by Jeff Kinney (2007), a three-pound text that is equally compelling for him, as all the boys in the class love to talk about Greg Heffley's antics.

- After learning about Jane Goodall, Kya, a first grader, decides that she, too, wants to grow up to study animals in their natural habitats. During guided reading, Kya reads from texts at Level G, so her teacher has gathered an assortment of small texts, ranging from Level E through Level H, about different wild animals. Each day, Kya reads and rereads some of these, regularly selecting new texts to add to the assortment as she narrows her interest in wild animals. Every few days, Kya also spends a little time in the Eyewitness book *Cat* (Clutton-Brock and King 1991), which includes sections about lions and tigers. Kya can figure out portions of this text. It pushes the limits, however, of a ten-pound text for her, so she compensates by spending time studying and learning from the pictures, much the way an athlete might stretch for a few minutes between weight-lifting intervals.

Third grader Aimee is interested in learning about snakes. During a conference with her teacher, she develops a plan for working through four texts, one after the other, that increase in difficulty, so that each text builds background knowledge for the next. On a given day, Aimee is reading from only one text, but over the course of a week she reads from all four just-right text weights. She begins the week with *Snakes: Strikers and Squeezers* (Evans 2008), a relatively easy book with short sentences, a lot of vocabulary support, and many color photographs. She wraps up the week with *Awesome Snake Science! 40 Activities for Learning About Snakes* (Blobaum 2012), a much longer book with some black-and-white photographs, considerably more complex sentences, and content-specific vocabulary.

We presented only a handful of scenarios, but there are many other ways to integrate different text levels across independent reading. We are certain you will come up with many we haven't even thought of. As you do, please evaluate your designs against a benchmark of simplicity, and let student engagement and joy serve as your indicators of success.

• • • Staying True to Our Intentions

Once again, we evaluate our lessons along the same principles that guided their development. The following sections consider the *Lifting Weights* lesson against our four intentions: alignment, balance, sustainability, and joy.

Intention 1: We intend toward alignment with our inner teacher.

Our inner teacher holds fast to the idea that in order to learn to read "independently and proficiently," students must have dedicated time to actually read . . . independently, no less! With its emphasis on productive effort, *Lifting Weights* is grounded in the assumption that independent reading is paramount to a reader's growth and success.

In addition, *Lifting Weights* gives educators a way to scaffold students less, without stifling their interests. *Lifting Weights* is a reasonable middle ground between saying, "Read whatever you want" and "Here are the Articles of Confederation. Read them." Based on our experiences with this lesson, this middle ground feels like home as we watch readers surprise themselves, their teachers, and us.

Because of the time necessary to teach some required "complex" texts, especially those that border on inappropriately difficult, efforts to align to the Common Core are, in many classrooms, taking over independent reading time. By focusing independent reading on productive effort, and by raising the expectations of students as they self-direct their experiences with text, we hope that the *Lifting Weights* strategy offers teachers validation for preserving—as well as a vocabulary for defending—independent reading practice. Our inner teacher feels relieved at the thought of your inner teacher getting what it wants. We like to imagine spontaneous eruptions of laughter and exclamations of wonder bubbling from your classroom as students read independently.

Intention 2: We intend toward balance.

Supporting students as they read to understand "complex literary and informational text independently and proficiently" (CCSS 2010)—is the backbone of this chapter, and really of this whole book. As the *Lifting Weights* lesson specifically teaches students the value of productive effort, it helps them manage complex texts. Because of the ways it teaches students to independently practice in heavy texts by reframing the problems they encounter as possibilities for developing muscle, *Lifting Weights* meets, even exceeds, our criteria for aligning to external standards.

Intention 3: We intend toward sustainability.

One valuable aspect of this lesson, in terms of sustainability, is the vocabulary it offers to classroom conversations around any interaction with a text. If we teach students this lesson's terminology as it relates to the *Lifting Weights* strategy—*weight, muscle, strength, form, productive effort*, and so on—then we have language for describing effort and text difficulty as they relate to most any text, from reading a social studies textbook to reading a poem for a shared reading experience. Furthermore, understandings of the ways productive effort and growth are connected hold the potential to influence student learning in any area, from music to math to sports.

By far the most powerful, sustainable benefit of *Lifting Weights*, however, is the way it reframes problems as possibilities, giving students agency. Not only does this lesson show students the ways they are powerful as readers, but by emphasizing the work of productive effort, it also makes learning an equal opportunity experience. When the emphasis in independent reading—even in terms of the social pressures of the classroom—is less about reading the thickest book and more about successfully taking on the maximum reading weight without compromising form, then the reader who struggles the most can begin to consider him- or herself a strong, agentive reader.

Once, when teaching the *Lifting Weights* lesson, Jan watched Leonard, a first grader, fight his way through a Level C book about monkeys. By traditional definitions, he was the most challenged reader in the classroom, but that day he became the reading equivalent of Mr. America. During whole-group sharing at the end of independent reading, Jan compared Leonard to a picture of a bodybuilder lifting 500 pounds, and the whole class erupted in spontaneous applause. We joyfully accept student reinventions of themselves as testimony to the sustainability of this lesson.

Intention 4: We intend toward joy.

Independent reading runs the risk of becoming a casualty of standards-based instruction. The prominence of dry, conceptually dense texts at the expense of joyful, self-selected, independent reading is making too many classrooms feel joyless. As a counterpoint, *Lifting Weights* gives students, and the teachers who love them, two ways to discover more in-school joy.

First, there is room in the *Lifting Weights* structure for a student to simply read for pleasure. Whether reading Mo Willems or Shel Silverstein, palpable joy is common when we give children time to discover books and authors they love. Nothing else, in our opinion, has the power to lure students into the hard work they must do to navigate the complex texts in their future. We prime students for the sophisticated work of reading the most complex texts when we make space for Brianna, a second grader, to laugh aloud as she reads *The Stinky Cheese Man and Other Fairly Stupid Tales* (Scieszka 1992), or for Davis, a fifth grader, to become misty eyed over *Where the Red Fern Grows* (Rawls 1961). Such contributions to readers, teachers, and classrooms would be enough for us to declare *Lifting Weights* "joy approved." But there is more.

In addition to the essential emotional connections with texts that arise from reading purely for pleasure, *Lifting Weights* supports students in discovering the joyful counterpoint to recreational reading: discovering that they are smarter than they thought. *Lifting Weights* teaches readers about *productive* effort, particularly how this effort changes as texts become more difficult. Consequently, *Lifting Weights* helps children discover their power, which is quintessentially joyful. In one classroom, after conferring with Kim about the ways he could step into the challenges of a ten-pound text, one third grader looked at her incredulously and said, "I didn't know I could do that."

● ● ● Closing Thoughts

This chapter repurposes the traditional metaphor that compares challenging exercise to challenging learning, and offers a specific strategy for using this metaphor to help students self-select texts representing a range of difficulty levels. Whether one is working out at the gym or trying to become more proficient at reading increasingly difficult texts, getting stronger requires productive effort. Teaching students to vary the difficulty level of the texts they read during independent reading helps them pay attention to their form, working to read well while building muscle. When children learn to embrace textual challenges, such as difficult and confusing plotlines, they begin to reframe problems as possibilities. This change in perspective can help develop not only children's reading independence and proficiency, but also their sense of agency.

●●● Questions for Reflection

1. What are your students learning about the relationship between productive effort and growth? How do you know?

2. How are your students learning to select books for themselves? What is working? What needs to change?

3. How does your students' text selection process contribute to their growing sense of agency?

4. What are you learning about? What connections are you noticing between your productive effort and your growth?

●●● For Further Reading

Opening Minds: Using Language to Change Lives by Peter H. Johnston (2012)

Mindset: The New Psychology of Success by Carol S. Dweck (2006)

The Daily 5, Second Edition: Fostering Literacy Independence in the Elementary Grades by Gail Boushey and Joan Moser (2014)

Genius: The Life and Science of Richard Feynman by James Gleick (1993)

Chapter 6

JOY—READING MORE FOR THE LOVE OF IT

Joy to the world. All the boys and girls. Joy to the fishes in the deep blue sea. Joy to you and me.

—HOYT AXTON

You are a first-grade teacher. It is October, and you and your students are immersed in a wealth of predictable and decodable texts. You work to round out their early reading experiences with a balance of incredible picture books and read-alouds that show them why they are working so hard to learn to read. Your six-year-old daughter, Lea, attends the school where you work and is engaged in beginning reading work that parallels that of your students. You spend your days trying to help the young readers in your classroom understand how and why to read, and your nights doing the same with the little girl who settles nightly onto your lap.

Of late, however, accountability pressures and district mandates have forced you to cut back on independent reading and read-aloud to make more time for the district's prescribed phonics lessons and their accompanying texts. Both your students and Lea are finding the labor of learning to read less and less compelling. You've noticed that they are increasingly disenchanted with the uninspired stories in their books—"The fat cat sat on the mat." Though you persist, they are distracted. In fact, at home one night, after insisting that Lea read to you from her assigned phonics reader instead of listening to you read *Time for Bed* (Fox 1997) for the thousandth time, Lea refuses to read at all. You both end the day frustrated. You are disappointed that Lea isn't progressing more quickly as a reader and that she is not cooperating. Lea is frustrated that you are spending so little time reading aloud to her and that bedtime "is not fun anymore."

One evening, after a long day at school and more bedtime protests from your Lea—"I don't want to read with you tonight!"—that make you question, again, whether you are equipped for parenthood, you decide to skip reading practice with Lea altogether and instead suggest that she select a book from her shelf and read on her own. Both of you are glad to have a break from reading together, which gives you pause as you head to your bedroom to work through the pile of unfolded laundry spread across your bed.

A few minutes later, you hear Lea laughing loudly as she reads aloud to herself. You pause your sock-matching task, sneak to her bedroom, and peer through the crack where the door is slightly ajar. Her toy lantern is projecting a star-filled sky onto her ceiling as Lea reads an Elephant and Piggie book to her wind-up Peter Rabbit, her plush puppy, and her oversized Curious George. She reads the text in each speech bubble several times, once to figure out the words and then to practice the voices, shifting her inflection with each one. She smiles the entire time, studies the pictures, and laughs spontaneously with each page. She is lost, both in joyful effort and in the antics of Elephant and Piggie. She finishes the book and immediately informs her audience that she is going to read it to them again. You watch, noticing that her "work" has never been so relaxed and that you have never heard her read so well.

Suddenly, Lea notices you. "I didn't know you were there," she says.

You go to her, sit on the side of her bed, and stroke her hair. "You liked that book, didn't you?"

She smiles and nods. You reach into the basket of books and pull out *Let's Go for a Drive!* (Willems 2012), another Elephant and Piggie book. She gasps with elation and bounces in her bed. "Can I read it now?" she asks. You nod, and leave the room as she opens the book with a giggle and begins talking to her stuffed friends. You overhear her say, "I have a big surprise for you! I get to read you *another* book about Elephant and Piggie!" as you write yourself a reminder: "Don't forget to take Elephant and Piggie to school tomorrow!"

♥ ♥ ♥

Although hard work and persistence are critical for readers to grow, great progress isn't always the result of hard work. In fact, sometimes readers make the most progress when they "work" less and enjoy reading more, as the preceding vignette illustrates. Just as we don't attend to our physical wellness by engaging only in strength training and never simply going for a walk in the woods, readers need constant exposure to the sheer joy of reading. If students aren't frequently displaying wonder, joy, and tenderness as they interact with texts, if they aren't carrying around favorite titles to reread portions aloud to a best friend during recess, if they aren't begging the librarian to purchase more titles written by a particular author, then you probably need to spend more time showing them the ways reading can bring them deep satisfaction, pleasure, and joy.

The scarcity, or even absence, of deep connections with books makes the task of becoming a better reader even harder, which makes the task of teaching reading harder, too. There are many forces (no, we didn't say evil forces, but if you want to read it that way, you can) coming to bear on schools and classrooms, and these forces not only diminish joy, but introduce alternative emotions, such as fear, stress, disappointment, and boredom. This chapter is about helping you reclaim, for yourself and for your students, the joy you can create by helping them discover the power of books. Throughout *Reading Wellness*, we have referred to the ways in which reading books has inspired, even changed, readers. From Jane Goodall's reading of *Tarzan of the Apes* in Chapter 1 to Myra's triumph with *James and the Giant Peach* in Chapter 5, reading's power is varied and seemingly endless. In the sections that follow, we explore in more depth *some* of the ways that reading makes us feel, grow, and change.

● ● ● Reclaiming Joy

When we read Martha Beck's *Finding Your Own North Star: Claiming the Life You Were Meant to Live* (2001), we met Melvin, a middle manager at IBM who "snapped awake at midlife" only to find himself "dazed, unhappy, and way off course" (xiii). Beck, who was his counselor, asked Melvin the questions she traditionally asks on first visits with new patients, particularly those plagued with the malaise that was so apparent with Melvin:

> *"Is there anything you do regularly that makes you forget what time it is?" "Do you laugh more in some situations than others?" "Tell me everything you remember about the best meal you've ever had."* (2)

Melvin, who thought he was about to receive advice on changing jobs midcareer, couldn't answer these questions. He was startled by the nature of Beck's inquiries, and then by the fact that they left him speechless. Finally, he responded with "I'm sorry, but I'll have to put together some data and get back to you on these questions" (2).

As we read *Finding Your Own North Star*, we too were stunned that we found the aforementioned questions so difficult to answer. Mired in the effort of consulting, blogging, and managing our households, we were writing together at 5:00 A.M. most mornings and reading professional materials into the night. We were not cultivating joy in our lives, and we were neglecting ourselves, which had serious repercussions for our families.

So, we began supporting each other in re-visioning our lives around moments that felt good. We scheduled more time with our families and set out on a mission to discover hobbies that distract and engage us—different work that felt like play, such as dancing and Pilates. We reminded each other of these new priorities relentlessly, and most important, we let go of some of our work. The payoff in joy has been dramatic, both for our work and for our play. In fact, our time away from work engaged in joyful distraction has contributed as much to the writing of this book as actually crafting the words. Our intentional efforts toward joy and balance continue, but they began by reading a book that changed us.

••• The Transformative Power of Books

Most of us have had experiences with books that have changed us in some way: a human interest article about a family adopting a child with special needs, a professional piece about how writing poetry with inmates reduced recidivism by 100 percent, or a poem about baby teeth in a tiny box as reminders of children now grown. Our emotional responses to these texts often lock them into our memories, so much so that we can even remember where we were when we read them. In *On Writing: A Memoir of the Craft* (2001), Stephen King explains, "You can't write until you've been flattened by a book" (141). We know, however, that being flattened by a book holds rewards even beyond the implications for writing, so helping children discover books that flatten them is a high calling.

Whether reading *Tough Boris* (Fox 1998) to give students a glimpse of our connection to all humanity, reading *A Day's Work* (Bunting 1997) to broaden their understandings of integrity and justice, or weepily sharing *Sophie's Masterpiece* (Spinelli 2004) for its insights into generosity and love, showing students the ways in which texts support deep feelings and deep thought is one of the greatest privileges of teaching.

Lately, though, it seems that this privilege is increasingly overlooked as we feel forced to make space in classrooms for texts that, presumably, prepare students for standardized tests. We suggest however, that reading wellness is measured by more than numbers.

••• What the Numbers Don't Tell Us

Nestled in the Lehigh Valley of eastern Pennsylvania is a small town called Roseto. Roseto was settled in the late 1800s by mostly illiterate, poor laborers who left a hard life of work in the marble quarries southeast of Rome, Italy, for a life of promise in the slate quarries of the northeastern United States. As the first immigrants arrived in Roseto, they worked to establish their new town, and soon more and more of their old friends joined them in the New World. Before long, the feel of the streets of Roseto mimicked the streets of home, with small shops, bakeries, and cafés filled with people conducting business and conversing in Italian. Life was highly characteristic of most immigrant towns in the United States in the first half of the twentieth century, except for one major difference: the people of Roseto were not suffering and dying from heart disease (Bruhn and Wolf 2004; Gladwell 2011).

In the mid-1900s, heart disease was the leading cause of death in men under the age of sixty-five in the United States; in Roseto, however, heart attacks were rare. The men (and women) of this Pennsylvania hamlet seemed to have somehow escaped the epidemic. In 1961, Stewart Wolf, a physician and medical school professor at the University of Oklahoma, decided to figure out why.

Wolf began combing through countless medical records of the residents of Roseto, collected samples of their blood, and administered EKGs, but the medical histories and test results couldn't explain why they were living so long. Wolf probed further. He investigated the fat and calorie content of their diets. He discovered that the people of Roseto cooked with lard and ate lots of fatty foods, such as sausage and pepperoni. Wolf was confounded.

One by one, Wolf eliminated diet, exercise, genes, and geography as variables contributing to the longevity enjoyed by Roseto's residents. No matter how he manipulated the data he collected, the numbers just did not explain the low occurrence of heart disease in Roseto. Frustrated, Wolf elicited the help of a colleague, who traveled with him across the country to spend time in Roseto, and then the mystery began to unravel. As Wolf and his colleague walked the streets, they observed people visiting one another and chatting in Italian. They noticed that in many households, three generations of family lived together. They saw that the people of Roseto gardened and shared vegetables with neighbors, made wine from grapes they grew, and planned festivals for drinking it. Not only did these people not suffer from heart disease, but there was hardly any poverty, suicide, drug addiction, or crime in their community. Why? Because of the quality of life in Roseto, which made its residents happy. They spent their time doing the things that made them feel good, things that created deep connections among them. These connections protected them from the pressures of the modern world, making them healthier.

• • • Giving Children Reasons to Read

Although we know that cooking with lard and eating a lot of sausage are not good ideas, at least in terms of heart health, the story of the people of Roseto illustrates the ways quality of life can confound traditional, even proven, understandings about health. The media, the general public, parents, and district administrators are watching classrooms, studying various assessment results, and powerfully influencing classroom cultures in ways that can negatively affect the quality of life in schools and classrooms. These influencers are largely well intentioned, but their efforts can actually interfere with learning, and even rob classrooms of joy.

Fortunately, great books are central to teaching children to read closely, making it easier to simultaneously communicate the joy of reading and align instruction to standards. Although there are paths to reading bliss with standards-based instruction, they are not necessarily obvious, and discovering them requires intention. To find these opportunities, point your compass toward joy and search for its many manifestations—laughter, tears, gasps—in the texts you offer students. Notice when it surfaces in your classroom, and dedicate yourself to squeezing as many meaningful text interactions into your day as possible.

In her book *In the Company of Children* (1996), Joanne Hindley tells a wonderful story about how her father had trouble learning to read. At the end of second grade, his teacher told his mother, Joanne's grandmother, that if he couldn't read all the stories in the second-grade reader by the end of the summer, he would have to repeat second grade. So, Joanne's grandmother took a stack of basal readers to their lake house, the family's regular summer retreat, where he sat on the screened porch and tried to sound out words while the other children in the neighborhood played in the water.

As his mother, who must have been experiencing extreme inner distress, watched him struggle, she began to wonder if the issue was less with her son and more with the books he was assigned. She went to the library and checked out a stack of "pocket westerns." Then, providing her son a brilliant, counterintuitive reading intervention, she read the books aloud to him, rather than making him read. In a moment of motherly alchemy, she turned reading practice from an arduous, lonely effort into an engaging, relaxed, intimate interaction with her. Joanne's grandmother turned lead into gold.

The catch, however, was that she stopped reading at the height of the excitement, such as when the gunslingers were poised at either end of the street. At these climactic points, Joanne's grandmother would set down the book, leaving to take care of something in the house. Sitting on the porch with those characters and stories waiting for him, Joanne's father couldn't resist picking up the books and persevering with the words to find out who won the gunfight or if the hero survived the rattlesnake bite. Joanne's father experienced the joy of reading success, the pleasure of understanding, and the power of stories, all from "working" less and enjoying more. In many classrooms around the country, it seems that we are practicing reverse alchemy, turning gold into lead. We find that in classrooms where celebrating wonderful books is at the heart of the classroom culture, the work of teachers and students is easier, more successful, and . . . well, more joyful.

●●● The *Feeling Good* Lesson Overview

The *Feeling Good* lesson begins with the teacher selecting a book that he or she loves, one that is a favorite for sharing with children. The teacher hugs the book, with the cover to his or her heart, so that the children can't see the title.

Figure 6.1
Kim opens a *Feeling Good* lesson by hugging a favorite book.

The teacher tells the children about how reading the particular book always makes him or her feel "really good," and then tells them a bit about why the book elicits these feelings. Next, the teacher reads the text aloud simply for pleasure, noticing aloud with students when the book obviously makes them feel the way the teacher anticipated it would make them feel. For example, if the teacher is sharing a book that makes him or her feel good because it is funny, the teacher would notice when the students are laughing and how laughing makes us feel good.

Next, the teacher creates a chart titled *Reading Makes Us Feel Good When . . .* and adds a descriptor related to the book that was just read aloud. Then the teacher shares two or three other books that make him or her feel good for other reasons and adds statements to the chart. Then, students read independently from self-selected texts, noticing the ways the books they are reading make them feel good. During independent reading, the teacher confers with students, helping them explore the different ways the books they are reading make them feel good. Finally, the students share with partners, and then some students share with the whole class. As students describe the different ways their books make them feel good, the teacher adds statements to the chart. We present the complete *Feeling Good* lesson in Table 6.1.

Table 6.1

The *Feeling Good* Lesson

PURPOSE	
LONG-RANGE PURPOSES	IMMEDIATE PURPOSES
● To help children learn to love reading ● To show children that there are many ways a book can make a reader feel good	● To help children find an intrinsic motivation to persist in the hard work of reading practice ● To help children find books and authors they love

continued

STANDARDS	TIME FRAME
Reading Anchor Standards: 1, 2, 10 Speaking and Listening Anchor Standards: 1, 4	20–30 minutes

MATERIALS

One book for reading aloud that is likely to make you and students feel good when you read it (see Table 6.2 for suggestions); two other favorite books that make you feel good for different reasons; chart paper and markers; books for each student to read independently (previously selected by students)

PROCEDURE AND PRACTICE

1. Gather the students, preferably on the floor or in a circle. Sit in front of them, hugging to your chest the book you are going to read aloud. Make sure students can't see the cover. Hug the book hard and smile long enough to arouse student curiosity.

2. Say something like, "I really love this book because when I read it, it makes me feel good. When I read this book, I laugh and laugh all the way through. And when I finish reading it, I want to go tell someone about it or read it all over again. This book makes me feel good because it is soooo funny!"

3. Show students the cover of the book and talk some more about the way the book makes you feel good, possibly referring to specific portions of the text. Then say something like, "This is just not fair, is it? I'm talking about how this book makes me feel good, and some of you may not have ever read it. I should read this aloud *now!*" Demonstrate enthusiasm over the opportunity to read this favored text.

4. Read the text aloud to students simply for pleasure. Notice aloud the ways the book elicits the predicted response. For example, if you said you love the book because it is funny, say something like, "I told you this book would make you laugh!" and "Isn't this book hilarious?!"

5. After reading the book, take a moment to let students respond to it. Reinforce students' noticings about how the book made them feel good.

continued

6. Take a piece of chart paper and write "Reading Makes Us Feel Good When . . ." at the top. Explain to students that you want them to help you notice all the ways books make readers feel good.

7. Add a statement to the chart related to the book you just read aloud. For example, if you read aloud a funny text, write something like, ". . . when it makes us laugh a lot" or ". . . when the book is very funny." See Figure 6.2 for an illustration.

8. Show students two other texts that make you feel good in ways that are different from the first text. Don't read these books aloud to the students but offer a brief description or use texts you have shared with the class previously. For a book such as *The Tenth Good Thing About Barney* (Viorst 1987) or *Where the Red Fern Grows* (Rawls 1961), you might say something like, "This book made me cry. It was really sad, but I still loved it. It made me feel good because it was written so well that it made me feel what the character felt." For a favorite informational text, you might say something like, "This book makes me feel good because I love to learn about outer space. This book has great pictures, and I can read and understand the words, so I learn a lot when I read from this book."

9. Add statements to the chart for each of these titles, such as ". . . when we feel what the character feels" or ". . . when we learn something new about something we are really interested in."

10. Send students off to read independently by telling them to be sure to notice the ways their books make them feel good. Let students read.

11. Confer with individual students who are engrossed in their reading. Start the conference by saying something such as, "Wow! You are really absorbed in your book, so it must feel really good to read it. How is your book making you feel good?" Let students read specific "feel-good" portions of their text to you, and celebrate with them the ways their book makes them feel good.

12. Gather students back together on the floor and/or in a circle. Let students talk with partners about the ways their books made them feel good. Call on some individuals to share their observations with the class. Add to the *Reading Makes Us Feel Good When . . .* chart as new noticings arise.

continued

NOTES

- Initially, students may not be very discerning, particularly young students. Everything makes them "feel good," which is okay. Help them articulate their noticings. They will get better at this with practice.

- The *Feeling Good* lesson is *not* a "feelings" lesson; rather it is a lesson about feeling good. There is a fine, but important, distinction between these concepts. Although a book may make the reader feel "happy," the lesson is about *why* the book makes the reader feel happy and how happiness feels good.

- Not every "good feeling" experience with text has to be profound or deep. We want students to have inspiring, even life-changing experiences with texts, but the good feelings that come from laughing with *Calvin and Hobbes* or figuring out a tricky spot in a guided reading text are valid and worth collecting as well.

- Each reader's emotional connections are his or her own. Try to avoid judgment. It is easy to think that the books that move us are better books or that certain types of experiences with texts are more important than others.

Figure 6.2
Sample *Reading Makes Us Feel Good When . . .* Chart

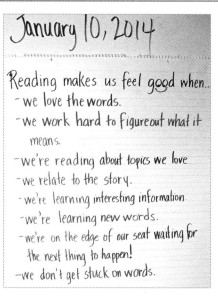

January 10, 2014

Reading makes us feel good when...
- we love the words.
- we work hard to figure out what it means.
- we're reading about topics we love.
- we relate to the story.
- we're learning interesting information.
- we're learning new words.
- we're on the edge of our seat waiting for the next thing to happen!
- we don't get stuck on words.

• • • Feeling Good Sample Lessons

The *Feeling Good* lesson is designed to help students think about the ways reading makes them feel good and to help perpetuate these good feelings, leading to more sustained, joyous reading. The sample *Feeling Good* lessons that follow help students think about other ways a text can make them feel good.

Sample Lesson 1: When Hard Work Feels Good

Books can make us feel good not only when their content is emotionally appealing, but when they help us accomplish something. Productive effort in a text feels good, too. This lesson helps students think about the ways their productive reading effort can make them feel good.

Start the lesson by hugging the directions for something, such as assembling a piece of furniture that comes in a box or a special recipe. Continue the lesson by saying something like this:

You're never going to believe the kind of reading material I'm hugging today. In a million years, I never would have imagined this kind of reading would make me feel good, but I have to tell you, this reading not only made me feel good, it made me feel great! [Reveal that you are holding the directions for making a lemon meringue pie, which is your father's favorite dessert.] I got this recipe from my aunt, who makes the best lemon meringue pie ever! I really wanted to make this recipe because it was my dad's birthday and I wanted to surprise him with his favorite dessert. I was very excited about making this pie, because I wanted to do something special for my dad. I knew he would be happy and touched. But then I saw the recipe! [Demonstrate your disappointment by dropping your shoulders and shaking your head.] I quickly discovered that lemon meringue pie is *hard* to make, which made me not so excited anymore! The recipe called for things that I had never even heard of, like "lemon zest" and "cream of tartar." Even though I knew it was going to be hard work to read and understand this recipe, I decided to give it a try. It's always good to at least try, right?

To gather the ingredients for the pie, I had to actually do research and read some other texts! Can you believe that? This was hard work, but it taught me things that I didn't even realize I needed to know. I learned about the tools that bakers use and how to make a piecrust. This research and all the extra reading actually made following the directions for the pie a lot easier, since it taught me words that were in the recipe, like *whisk* and *crimp* and *simmer*. But knowing these words still didn't make following the directions for making the pie *easy*.

Well, I stuck with it. And do you know what? I made that pie for my dad. It was not perfect, of course. The crust was burnt, and there were some lumps in the lemon filling, but I was still very proud. Now when I see this recipe, I still think about how hard I worked, and that helps me know that I can work hard to read other difficult texts.

I've had other experiences when it felt good to read something that was hard for me to understand, such as when I had to read the directions to put together a bookshelf that came in a box. Oh, my goodness! That was really hard. Or when I had to read the directions for programming my phone. All of these reading experiences gave me good feelings, even though the reading material itself wasn't exactly exciting.

Ask students if they have ever read something hard in order to do something they wanted to do. Let students share their responses with the group. Review with the students the *Reading Makes Us Feel Good When . . .* chart. Add sentence endings based on the day's discussion. They might look something like this:

> ". . . when it helps us do something we want to do."

> ". . . when we think we can't do something, but then we figure it out."

> ". . . when we can cook/build/make something because we read the directions."

> ". . . when it shows us that we are getting smarter."

Conclude the lesson by reminding students to continue to look for examples of texts that make them feel good because the texts help them learn how to do something or figure something out.

Sample Lesson 2: How We Read Can Make Us Feel Good

Another of the many ways books can make you feel good is by sharing them with others. Oftentimes the *way* we experience a text contributes as much to our good feelings as the text itself. For example, in a first-grade classroom, repeated choral readings of *Brown Bear, Brown Bear, What Do You See?* (1996) by Bill Martin Jr. create all kinds of warm associations with this classic, patterned text. Such "corporate" readings of favorite books build community and loving associations—i.e., good feelings—with texts (Holdaway 1979).

Other examples of the ways entire reading experiences can contribute to feeling good include reading a bedtime story to a child in a rocking chair, sharing a young adult novel with a teenager chapter by chapter over breakfast each morning, or reclining on the beach as you read a long-awaited title by your favorite author. In these cases, the total reading experience, as much as the text, contributes to positive associations with the book and makes the reader feel good.

You can modify the lesson description in Table 6.1 to introduce texts that you love, at least in part, because of your memories of *how* you read them. These memories might include connections to *who* you read the book with or *where* you were when you read it. Possible language follows here.

Today I want to continue our conversation about the way reading makes us feel good. Let's look back over all the ways we've listed that books give us good feelings. [Refer to your *Reading Makes Us Feel Good When . . .* chart.] I've been thinking a lot about when reading makes me feel good, and I discovered something. Sometimes, it's not just the book that makes me feel good. Sometimes, it's *how* I read the book or *where* I read the book that makes me feel good.

For example, when my son Nathan was little, he couldn't get enough of this book *Where the Wild Things Are* [Sendak 1963]. He wanted to read it every single night, and I would cuddle him up and read it to him. He and I both eventually memorized it. Not only did we love the book, but we loved being together. Reading it every night was our special time together. Now I can just look at *Where the Wild Things Are* and I have good feelings. Memories of cuddling up with my son when he was little come back to me, as do favorite lines from the book. We used to always say, "And Max said, 'I'll eat you up!'" together.

Another book that makes me feel good—not just because of the book, but also because of my experiences with it—is *Charlotte's Web* [White 1952]. Remember when I read that aloud to you and how excited we were to read another chapter every day? That was so much fun, wasn't it? We loved the book, but we also loved reading it together as a classroom community. Now whenever I look at *Charlotte's Web*,

I think about you and how lucky I am to get to read to you every day.

I know we've talked today about reading experiences with other people, and how these experiences can feel good and make a book special, but sometimes reading a book alone can feel especially good because of where or how we read it. When I was your age, I loved to read Nancy Drew mysteries. [Show students a book from the series.] I would read them at night, under the covers, with a flashlight. They were a little bit scary—not so scary that I couldn't sleep, but scary enough to make me want to keep reading. I used to love to get into bed at night to make a tent out of my covers and read Nancy Drew books. Now I get up early in the morning to read by myself. I light a candle, make a cup of coffee, and read books that I think I might fall in love with. These books often become very special to me. So, you can have good feelings about a reading experience when you read by yourself, too.

Give students time to think about reading experiences similar to the ones you describe, and then let them share their thoughts with partners. Call on a few students to share their special reading experiences with the whole group. Add statements to the *Reading Makes Us Feel Good When . . .* chart. Here are some possible additions:

". . . when we read with someone we love."

". . . when we read a book over and over."

". . . when we read in special places."

". . . when a book is so good, we want to tell our friends about it."

". . . when a book is so good, we read it instead of doing work we need to do."

Close the lesson by asking students to continue thinking about how the ways they read can make them feel good. Encourage them to take care of themselves by thinking about where and how they are reading. What changes can they make to make their reading experiences as enjoyable as possible?

••• Student Conferences and *Feeling Good*

Although the introductory lesson described in Table 6.1 teaches children to think about the ways reading makes them feel good, the heart of *Feeling Good* is the individual conferences you will have with students. We are amazed by the insights we gain during these conferences, both into the ways reading makes individual students feel good and into each student's reading process. During conferences we prompt students with open-ended statements and questions such as "How is your reading today making you feel good?" and "Please, read me a part of your book that really made you feel good and tell me *why* it made you feel good." These questions tend to draw thoughtful responses from students.

Consider Eva, a fifth grader, who was reading a book about a girl who had recently moved and was attending a new school. In a conference, Kim asked Eva how her reading was making her feel good. Eva said she could relate to the main character, and she carefully looked through her book to share an excerpt of the character talking to her friend about moving.

When Kim asked Eva, who had lived her entire life in the same house, to explain how she related to this section, Eva said that it wasn't the part about moving that spoke to her, but how this character dealt with moving. Because moving was a source of angst for the character, she relied on the support of her best friend to help her work through her anxiety. As Eva pointed this out, she said, "I'm just like her. When I have problems, I talk to my best friend, and she always makes me feel better." Eva connected to the story because it showed her that she is not alone. Her response not only showed that Eva comprehended an important theme of the book, but it also revealed something important about her as a person—that her connections with her friends help her navigate the angst of childhood. Such revelations are valuable not only because they provide teachers with information about *how* a child reads, but also because they tell us much about *who* each child is.

• • • More Titles for *Feeling Good* Lessons

The titles in Table 6.2 represent a variety of ways books can make readers feel good. We are partial to picture books for *Feeling Good* lessons, even for upper elementary students, because picture books are universally appealing and because they are manageable in a single sitting, quickly and powerfully communicating your message. Although not included in this list, longer texts also work for *Feeling Good* lessons, particularly if students are familiar with the text. If you select a chapter book or other lengthy text for a *Feeling Good* lesson, simply share excerpts that illustrate the way the book might make readers feel good. This list is by no means exhaustive! Rather, there are many, many more ways that reading feels good, and we expect that you will discover them with your students.

Table 6.2

Sample Texts for *Feeling Good* Lessons

TITLE	POSSIBLE ADDITIONS TO THE *READING MAKES US FEEL GOOD WHEN . . .* CHART
Press Here by Hervé Tullet (2011) *What Animals Really Like* by Fiona Robinson (2011)	". . . when the book is interactive."
One by Kathryn Otoshi (2008) *Because Amelia Smiled* by David Ezra Stein (2012)	". . . it makes us want to be better people."

continued

Green Eggs and Ham by Dr. Seuss (1960) *Rachel Fister's Blister* by Amy MacDonald (1993)	". . . when the words roll off our tongues or make us read along."
Snow Day! by Lester Laminack (2010) *The Sweetest Fig* by Chris Van Allsburg (1993)	". . . when the ending is unexpected."
The Lego Ideas Book by Daniel Lipkowitz (2011) *Family Fun Super Snacks* by Deanna F. Cook (2004)	". . . when it helps us get better at something we love to do."
Zen Ties by Jon J. Muth (2008) *Inch by Inch* by Leo Lionni (1960)	". . . when it changes the way we think."
Guess How Much I Love You by Sam McBratney (2008) *The Kissing Hand* by Audrey Penn (1993)	". . . when it shows us what love is."
Come On, Rain! by Karen Hesse (1999) *What You Know First* by Patricia MacLachlan (1998)	". . . when the words are beautiful."
I Know Here by Laura Croza (2010) *Where the Wild Things Are* by Maurice Sendak (1963)	". . . when it shows us that other people have the same feelings we have."
The Carrot Seed by Ruth Krauss (1945) *Wilfrid Gordon McDonald Partridge* by Mem Fox (1984)	". . . when the child in the story is wiser than the grown-ups."

• • • More Ways to Teach *Feeling Good*

Once you and your students begin to examine texts for the ways they make you feel good, you are likely to find that joyous, engaged reading increases in your classroom. The more you look at emotionally rich texts together, the better students will become at identifying the ways different books make them feel different kinds of good feelings. Perpetuating these feelings means that students, and you, actually spend more time during your day feeling good. This can give you energy for your work and strengthen your classroom community.

Feeling Good lessons also naturally connect to conversations about comprehension monitoring, because readers have to understand texts in order to enjoy the ways they make them feel good. Feeling good while reading is a sign that students are comprehending what they are reading, and you can teach students to notice and appreciate this connection.

To help you build your classroom community, to perpetuate good feelings across the school day, and to help students understand the ways feeling good is an indicator of comprehension, we offer you three lesson extensions.

Celebrate North Star reading experiences.

As we've described throughout this chapter, books evoke a range of emotions— or ways of feeling good. We want you and your students to experience the profound connections to books that are possible, the connections that are "as deep as a love affair" (Lehman and Roberts 2014, 2). Whereas Sample Lesson 2 teaches children that the context of a reading experience can contribute to their good feelings about the book, this extension introduces children to the idea that sometimes a reading experience is so powerful, it changes us.

Begin by talking with students about the books and reading experiences that you have found most powerful, even life changing. We think of these texts as "North Stars" because they, combined with the whole of our experience reading them, help us find our way through life. Oftentimes, North Star books represent the pinnacle of our reading experiences, combining the good feelings that come from discovering that a particular text says just what we need it to say just when we need to hear it with the fact that it speaks in similar ways to someone we love. A reader's joy is high and memories are cemented when there is simultaneous meaning around the *who*, *what*, and *when* of an experience with text. In the paragraphs that follow, we describe a couple of our own recent North Star reading experiences.

In the process of moving from the house she imagined she would grow old in—a house filled with memories of the entire childhoods of both her sons—Kim read with her family *What You Know First* (MacLachlan 1998), which is a child's story of how she collects memories before leaving the home that has been in her family for generations. Even though Kim had read it many times and long appreciated its beauty and depth, *What You Know First* became a North Star text for her in the moment that she read it with her sons and then walked with them from room to room of their home, remembering with tears and laughter the years lived in each dear space.

Similarly, Jan has read Sandra Cisneros's story "Eleven" (1991) in many contexts over many years. When she sat on the couch with one arm wrapped around her son, Natie, on the day after his eleventh birthday, however, and read "Eleven" aloud, the *who*, *what*, and *when* of the story turned the reading into a dear memory. With the very first sentence—"What they don't understand about birthdays and what they never tell you is that when you're eleven, you're also ten, and nine, and eight, and seven, and six, and five, and four, and three, and two, and one" (6)—Natie was captivated, and Jan reflected on the bittersweetness of his accumulating years.

Such powerful experiences with text are not everyday occurrences. When you or your students have North Star experiences with books—those experiences that give them direction or energy or love or something else—celebrate and share them as reading rites of passage. Create classroom rituals around North Star books, such as letting students write the title on a rock and adding it to a totem in your classroom or reverentially positioning the book in a display of North Star books in your classroom. Most of all, let children write about and talk about these experiences, so that they remember them vividly and can use them as guides for discovering more texts that are important, even life changing, for them.

Build classroom community.

Mark Twain's assertion that in order "to get the full value of a joy you must have somebody to divide it with" (1989, 241) proves true with *Feeling Good* lessons. Student conversations about how books make them feel good build classroom community in ways that mini-lessons and teacher testimonials cannot. For example, when Tracy and Brennan trade out books in the Origami Yoda series by Tom Angleberger, they read aloud favorite parts to each other and each predict how the other will react to the text: "You're going to love the part when . . . !" Such connections between students can enhance the quality of students' reading life, helping your classroom become more and more like Roseto, Pennsylvania.

Explore ways to further student conversations about books. For example, let children use sticky notes to put messages in the front of books that make them feel good. Explain to students that when they read a book that makes them feel good, they can sign their name, list the page number of a favorite section, and make comments, such as "Read this book right NOW!" In the same way that we are excited to go to the local, independent bookstore to find titles recommended by our favorite store clerks, your students will be excited about finding the notes left by their friends, as well as about adding notes of their own.

Connect *Feeling Good* to comprehension monitoring.

As we mentioned earlier, emotional responses to texts also indicate that a reader is comprehending. For example, if a student laughs out loud when a text is funny, it indicates that he or she has comprehended it. Students must read texts well in order to enjoy maximum good feelings.

You can help students make the connection between the way a text makes them feel and comprehension monitoring by sharing a text with students that is sure to elicit a strong emotional response—i.e., something hilarious, sad, gross, and so on. Let students talk with partners to try to identify exactly *why* the text evokes such strong emotion. Refer to specific comprehension strategies that you have taught and that students naturally integrate as they respond to texts emotionally. For example, a funny text usually requires students to simultaneously connect to their background knowledge, visualize, and infer.

Help students notice the ways they are using *many* reading strategies at once whenever they have an emotional reaction to a text. Limit strategy discussions, as strategy use is not an end in itself!

During a conference, one fourth-grade girl named Deanna was reading *39 Clues* by Rick Riordan (2008). She said that her reading wasn't making her feel anything in particular. When probed, she explained, "It makes me feel odd." Further conversation revealed that she was confused by the text because she was skipping over the words that she did not know and making no attempt to figure them out. When asked what she was going to do, she said she could either "go back" or "read on." As she began to apply the reading strategies she already knew, her face lit up. "Oh, I get it," she whispered to herself. By the end of the conference, Deanna was feeling good in several different ways that she was able to articulate. She was "proud" that she figured out the words that she had skipped, she was engaged in the story because it no longer felt "odd," and she had a new sense of agency because she realized that she had strategies she could use.

After watching a *Feeling Good* lesson, one second-grade teacher marveled at how her students demonstrated their comprehension as they described the ways their books made them feel good. "So many of their understandings were connected to their good feelings," she said to Jan with amazement, "and so much of their comprehension came from the sheer joy of loving what they were reading."

• • • Staying True to Our Intentions

In the sections that follow, we examine this final *Reading Wellness* lesson to see how well it addresses our four intentions. Not surprisingly, we found it easy to identify the ways the *Feeling Good* lesson meets our expectations for alignment, balance, sustainability, and, most obviously, joy.

Intention 1: We intend toward alignment with our inner teacher.

The *Feeling Good* lesson serves as a reminder that all is lost if we teach children how to read but fail to show them *why* to read. By design, the *Feeling Good* lesson feels good to teach, which of course gives our inner teacher—who also wrestles with the dissonance around preparing students for high-stakes tests—peace. Even more, our inner teacher is happier still at the thought of you discovering the ways great books are a pathway to increased joy and peace in the classroom. While listening to and laughing through a read-aloud of an Elephant and Piggie book during a *Feeling Good* lesson, one second grader put his hand on his chest and said, "My heart is just getting bigger and bigger!" Nothing pleases our inner teacher more than this sort of spontaneous display of reading joy.

Intention 2: We intend toward balance.

Although our primary motivation is alignment with our inner teacher, which in this chapter involves advocating for students to spend more time feeling good as they interact with texts, we cannot overlook the other instructional responsibilities entrusted to us. We must teach children to read closely and comprehend deeply. We must give them opportunities to develop fluency and support their growing proficiency with phonics and word analysis. Thus, we have to make sure that we explicitly teach comprehension, fluency, word analysis, and so on.

Feeling Good represents the backbone of "independence and proficiency." As readers are thinking about what "feels good" about their reading, they are synchronizing many skills that allow them to read closely and carefully as they draw logical inferences from texts.

Intention 3: We intend toward sustainability.

The *Feeling Good* lesson reminds us that reading serves its own purposes, and that it has intrinsic value—including the value of feeling good—apart from performance standards. We find that books can say more for themselves than we can say about them. If we get out of their way, as *Feeling Good* demonstrates, books can help readers become more skilled, furthering their independence and proficiency in ways that make our mini-lessons impotent by comparison. In fact, we think that a single, powerful, agentive experience with a wonderful book holds the potential to influence student fluency, comprehension, and reading stamina more than pages and pages of teacher talk. Such experiences with books support the self-extending nature of reading, offering the ultimate in sustainable benefits. That is, the realization that reading can make the reader feel good can lead to more reading, which leads to more successful experiences with text.

After a *Feeling Good* lesson and some dedicated time for independent reading, Jasmine, a second grader, shared how much she had learned from her book about spiders, referring to a specific page she had found fascinating. With contagious enthusiasm, she said to her classmates, "I just have to give this page a hug because I learned so much on it." In a similar situation, Cedric, a fourth grader, talked about his reading from *The Worst Case Scenario Survival Handbook (Junior Edition)* by David Borgenicht (2007). In addition to his obvious fascination with the text, he connected this interest to his increased proficiency. "I've read this so many times because I like it," he explained, "and I'm getting faster and faster."

We are by no means suggesting that you abandon mini-lessons and other explicit instruction, or that you simply let students have "fun" with books. We are suggesting, however, that explicit instruction has reached a critical mass in classrooms. We think it is appropriate, even essential—and certainly sustainable—to *also* create space for letting books teach students and for letting students teach themselves and each other, even if this means we have less time for explicit instruction.

Intention 4: We intend toward joy.

We were intentional about putting this, the "joy chapter," at the end of *Reading Wellness*. We put it last not because it is least important, but because we wanted it to be our "final word." If *Reading Wellness* influences the way you teach and live in and out of the classroom in no other way, we hope it makes you advocate for your right to live a life filled with joy. If you search for and create opportunities for *yourself* to experience more joy, you will inevitably bring more joy into the lives of your students.

When we demonstrate *Feeling Good*, holding a beloved text to our hearts as wide-eyed, curious children scooch closer and closer around our feet for a glimpse of the cover, everything is as it should be. In these moments, we know that students are about to engage in joyful experiences with text even as they learn about their reading processes. We are excited about you having more and more such moments in your classroom, too, and we are confident that they will give you—and your inner teacher—renewed energy, joy, and passion for the loving and important work you do with students.

Closing Thoughts

Helping readers discover the ways reading makes them feel good—whether laughing out loud, seeing their humanity in stories, or envisioning their futures—can powerfully influence the quality of life in a classroom. These emotional connections with books serve as a secret ingredient to increasing students' independence and proficiency as they camouflage hard work with joy. The resulting energy and passion, and the inevitable social connections, remind readers that reading is pleasurable and that it serves *their* purposes. This benefit reminds us that sometimes, working less and enjoying more is a viable path to progress. Giving children (and ourselves) permission to feel good often, and showing them that books are a reliable source for these good feelings, creates an environment in which students are more likely to discover the texts that are powerful for them, a discovery that holds promise for a lifetime of joy.

Questions for Reflection

1. How does the reading experience change for your students when it is joyful?

2. How well does your classroom library represent different ways of feeling good? What do you need to add to your library?

3. How can you and your students feel good in your classroom even more often?

4. In what ways do the books you read make you feel good? How do you find them? How do you share them? How can you bring more of these good-feeling books into your life?

5. What do you *love* to do? How can you do more of it?

● ● ● For Further Reading

Reading Magic: Why Reading Aloud to Our Children Will Change Their Lives Forever by Mem Fox (2008)

Finding Your Own North Star: Claiming the Life You Were Meant to Live by Martha Beck (2001)

How Reading Changed My Life by Anna Quindlen (1998)

Why Read? Mark Edmundson (2004)

The Happiness Project: Why I Spent a Year Trying to Sing in the Morning, Clean My Closets, Fight Right, Read Aristotle, and Generally Have More Fun by Gretchen Rubin (2009)

MATTERS OF CONSEQUENCE

If you were to say to the grown-ups: "I saw a beautiful house made of rosy brick, with a geranium in the windows and doves on the roof," they would not be able to get any idea of that house at all. You would have to say to them: "I saw a house that cost $20,000." Then they would exclaim: "Oh what a pretty house that is!"

—ANTOINE DE SAINT-EXUPÉRY

In the beloved children's classic *The Little Prince,* a man crashes his airplane in the Sahara. He wakes to find a little prince from another planet with him in the desert. The little prince anxiously explains that on his home planet, there is a rosebush that he loves and has left behind. The prince is afraid that his sheep will eat his beloved rosebush in his absence, and he grows increasingly distraught at the prospect of the bush's demise.

The pilot, distracted by his efforts to repair his plane and concerned for his own survival, is annoyed by the prince. In ever more distress, the little prince asks the pilot a barrage of questions in an effort to find out what the pilot believes about the fate of the rosebush. The pilot responds with frustration: "'No, no, no! I don't believe anything. I answered you with the first thing that came into my head. Don't you see—I am very busy with matters of consequence!'" (de Saint-Exupéry 1943, 28).

● ● ●

Teachers wrestle with distributing instructional time among competing "matters of consequence." Even under scrutiny and pressure to adhere to linear and categorical models of instruction, there remains a commitment among teachers to teach children to think—about words, ideas, stories, even about challenging concepts such as justice or peace or the ways they plan to change the world. The complication, of course, is that district, state, and even federal instructional directives focus largely on discrete content rather than on ways of thinking and knowing. "Others" have decided that particular instructional standards are the matters of consequence in classrooms. And the district, state, and federal others are interested in numbers—percentiles, rates, and scores.

Much like the quote from *The Little Prince* that opens this epilogue, teachers say to the others, "I have a student who loves to read. He has favorite authors, and he carries books with him everywhere. He reads when no one asks him to. When I see him, he begs to read me his favorite passages. He laughs and cries at the places the author intended, and he is happiest when he is reading. Will you come meet him?"

But the others cannot get an idea of the boy at all. They do not understand. The teachers have to say to them, "There is a child in my class who scored in the ninety-eighth percentile in reading on the standardized test." Then the others would exclaim, "Oh, what a smart child! We want to meet him! You are a wonderful teacher!"

While many of us fight to preserve instruction that is rich and deep, we cannot escape the details of measures and the public pressures of others. We are overwrought by rubrics. We are in a quandary over questions that are essential. Rather than deciding not to believe in *anything,* we find points of instructional meaning, even when the directives we receive make little sense. We continue to read beautiful books, ask questions that don't have one answer, and show children ways to think about tremendous and transformative ideas. But we feel pressure to teach as if we are preparing for some timed physical fitness test on live television, rather than continually working toward more and more wellness. We sometimes find it hard to think about anything else. This might please the others, but it doesn't do much for the boys and girls, or the teachers.

If we say to the most beleaguered teachers, "Read this book. It might change your life or the lives of your students," they are overwhelmed. But if we say to these teachers, who have almost forgotten that they love children's literature and open-ended conversation, "Teaching with this picture book will help your students meet reading standard 3," then they respond with relief. "Ahhhh!" they say. They do not believe that creative thinking is unimportant. But they are tired and searching for a way to satisfy the others while also honoring themselves and the students for whom they work.

The little prince begins to sob as he imagines the violence the sheep might commit against his rosebush, and the pilot realizes his insensitivity and describes his thoughts:

> *The night had fallen. I had let my tools drop from my*
> *hands. Of what moment now was my hammer, my bolt,*
> *or thirst, or death? On one star, one planet, my planet,*
> *the Earth, there was a little prince to be comforted.*
> *I took him in my arms, and rocked him.*
> (de Saint-Exupéry 1943, 31)

Sometimes, when it seems that the educational leaders and policy makers have gone amok, we are inclined to let instructional standards drop from our hands and ask, "Of what moment now are standards or rubrics or standardized tests?

We want students to develop literate identities and articulate their own important understandings. We have to teach them to feel, to think, to love, to question, to connect, and to create proficiently." This is the truth.

But we see the other truth, too. We often understand the efforts of the others, working to help us teach intentionally, analyze the instructional standards, and look critically at how our teaching translates into learning. Most educators see the value of educational standards. Who is not in favor of focusing instruction, of aligning what we teach with what we test, or of lifting our expectations of students? Who doesn't want *all* children to become proficient and independent readers? And this, too, is the truth.

So we have to figure out how to marry both worthwhile endeavors: teaching the instructional standards *and* teaching everything else. We have to make a hard case for read-aloud, for dialogic discussions, for social justice, for lifelong learning, for teaching children to think, for talking before writing, and for showing children in lots of different ways that *they* are matters of consequence. We need to articulate both a rationale and practical ideas for teaching children the instructional standards while also doggedly defending creativity, independent thought, higher-order thinking, joy, and everyone's right to change the world.

For all of us who are dedicated to thinking of students' reading development holistically rather than simply as data points, we know it is not enough to produce children who can read whatever "grade-appropriate, complex" text we set in front of them. Our visions for independence and proficiency are larger than college and career readiness. We stand beside you, imagining readers who *want* to read, *seek* to read, *need* to read.

Our intent for the six lessons that fill this book is to help readers move beyond the expectations of the others—to read closely, to identify the main idea, to notice how characters change, and so on—to *also* read for their own purposes, saying to themselves,

> "I can learn about things that interest me."

> "This is hard, but I can do it."

> "I will never be the same because I read this."

> "I want to share this with someone."

> "I don't want to stop reading."

We know that there are many paths to wellness, and that one's personal journey toward wellness never ends. We encourage you to vary and adapt the lessons in this book as you consider what *you* and your students need in order to become increasingly well. If you don't love the books we love, search for titles that move *you*. As you discover aspects of wellness that we don't address, please pursue them. Ultimately, it is up to *you* to imagine what wellness looks like for you and your students and to discover the paths that can make your vision a reality. Just as our thinking and writing developed from rich seeds planted by thinkers such as Martha Beck, Carol Dweck, Peter Johnston, and Richard Allington, we invite you to reinvent and build upon the ideas we share in this book.

We are honored that you have made the journey through *Reading Wellness* with us. As you teach the lessons in this book and support agentive reading and thinking in your classroom, we wish you much, much wellness. You are agents of reading joy, and we are with you.

Graphic Organizer for *Heart, Head, Hands, and Feet* Lessons

Name _____

Date _____

 **APPENDIX B**

Text Excerpts and Encryption for *Does That Match?* Lessons

In the pages that follow, we offer several different texts to choose from for the *Does That Match?* lessons, including those for beginning readers. First, we present the encrypted version of each text/excerpt, formatted for sharing with students. These handout versions are followed by the traditional versions of each passage to use as a key.

• ➤

● ● ● Part 1: Handout Versions

Grade 1

"Dinner" by Jan Burkins and Kim Yaris

I like to eat ♏♑♑⬧ for breakfast.

I like to ♏♋⧫ soup for lunch.

I like to eat ❍♏♋⧫ for dinner.

But I like to eat ice ♍❒♏♋❍ all the time!

Reading Wellness: Lessons in Independence and Proficiency by Jan Miller Burkins and Kim Yaris.
Copyright © 2014. Stenhouse Publishers.

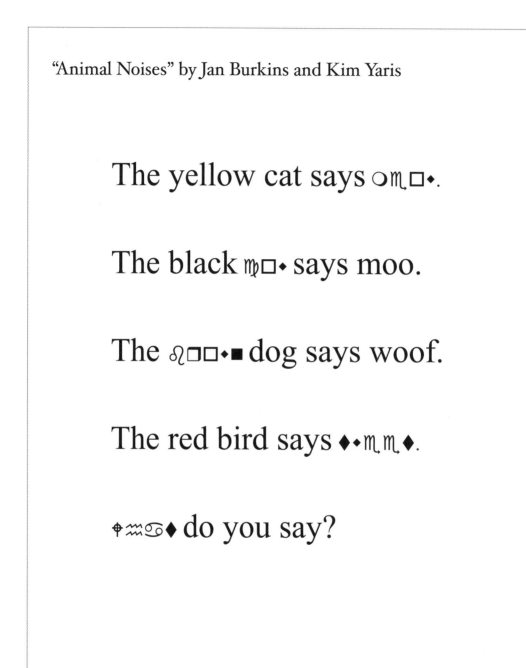

"Animal Noises" by Jan Burkins and Kim Yaris

The yellow cat says ○ɱ□◆.

The black ɱ□◆ says moo.

The ♌□□◆■ dog says woof.

The red bird says ◆◆ɱɱ◆.

◈ⵕ☊◆ do you say?

From *Hi! Fly Guy* by Tedd Arnold (2005):

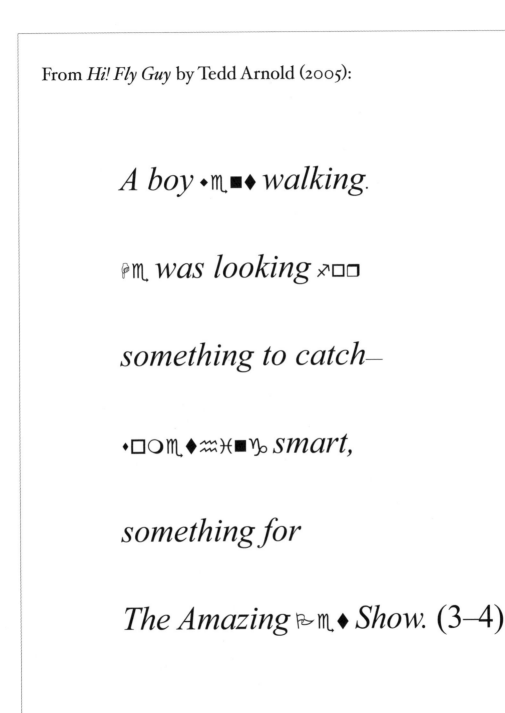

A boy ◆m■◆ walking.

☞m was looking ⤢□□

something to catch–

◆□○m◆≈X■♈ smart,

something for

The Amazing ☞m◆ Show. (3–4)

Grades 2–3

From *Soupy Saturdays with the Pain & the Great One*
by Judy Blume (2007):

> *On Saturdays we do errands with Dad. He's*
> *good at* ⬚⬚⬚⬚⬚⬚*. Today, even though*
> *it was really warm, the Pain was* ⬚⬚⬚⬚⬚⬚
> *earmuffs. Big fluffy ones.*
>
> *Our first stop was the* ⬚⬚⬚ *store. The shoe*
> *salesman took one look at the Pain and said,*
> *"We have some nice snow* ⬚⬚⬚⬚ *on sale.*
> *Half price." "Why would I want snow* ⬚⬚⬚⬚
> *in May?" the Pain asked.*
>
> *The shoe man* ⬚⬚⬚⬚⬚⬚*. "Looks like*
> *you're getting* ⬚⬚⬚⬚ *for winter," he said,*
> *pointing to the Pain's earmuffs.*
>
> *"I'm getting ready for a* ⬚⬚⬚⬚⬚⬚⬚*," the*
> *Pain told him.*
>
> *"Oh," the shoe salesman said, as if that*
> *made perfect* ⬚⬚⬚⬚*.*
>
> *The Pain got a pair of* ⬚⬚⬚⬚⬚⬚*. So did I.*
> (5–7)

Reading Wellness: Lessons in Independence and Proficiency by Jan Miller Burkins and Kim Yaris.

From *The Best Book of Spaceships* by Ian Graham (1998):

♦□☊♏♏♏ Suits

In space there is no air. Anything the Sun

♦♒♓■♏♦ on is boiling hot, and anything

in the ♦♒☊♏♏ is freezing cold. Human

beings cannot live in space. We need air to

♌□♏☊♦♒♏, and we need to be at the right

♦♏□♏□☊♦♦□♏—not too hot and not too

cold.

A spacecraft has to provide ☊♦□□■☊♦♦

with air to ♌□♏☊♦♒♏, and it has to keep

them warm. When astronauts leave the

♦□☊♏♏□□☊↗♦, they must wear a space

suit, which does the same job. (20)

Grades 4–5

From *My Life in Dog Years* by Gary Paulsen (1998):

Fred came to me in a small cardboard box

filled with wood ▯≋⊁▯◆*.*

I had been in a bookstore in Bemidji,

Minnesota, looking for a book on pickling fish.

I love to eat ▯⊁▥&♂●▥⚊ *herring and had*

access to a large supply of small northern pike.

It was in this uncomplicated frame of mind

that I met Fred.

I was at the curb when a small boy came up

to me holding an old detergent box.

"Hey, mister," he said with the air of a con

man, "you want to buy a ▯◆▯▯⬓*?"*

"Buy?" I stopped and □ℳℳ□ℳ♎ *into the box. There was nothing but a pile of wood shavings. "What puppy?"*

"He's in there, down in the ◆□□♎*. Dig him out.*

I dug around in the ◆♒♋❖✠■♈◆ *until my fingers hit the soft fur. There was a moment's hesitation, then a small growl; then a set of needle-sharp teeth* □✠□□ℳ♎ *into the soft tip of my finger.*

"He bit me!"

The boy ■□♎♎ℳ♎*. "He's half Lab and half something that came into the yard one night. Dad said he'd make a great watchdog."*
(90–91)

From *Immigrant Kids* by Russell Freedman (1980):

Many ⸎⚪⚪⸎⸎⬡⚆◼♦⬩ worked from home.
Tenement apartments became busy workshops
where entire ⸎⚆⚪⸎●⸎ⴳ⬩ labored seven days
a week ⬩⸎♦⸎■ⴳ clothing, making artificial
flower rolling cigars, ⬩≋⸎●●⸎■ⴳ nuts for
restaurants, and performing other low-paying
tasks. Children ⬩⬜⬜&⸎⚑ alongside their
parents from the time they were old enough to
⸎⬜●●⬜⬩ directions. Sometimes extra workers
were hired, and the ⚆⬜⚆⬜♦⚪⸎■♦ became
a small factory called a "sweatshop" because
of the ●⬜■ⴳ hours, hard work, and ●⬜♦ pay.
It was not unusual to find a dozen or more
⬜⸎⬜⬜●⸎—men, women, and children—at
work in a stuffy tenement room. (45)

● ● ● Part 2: Traditional Versions

Grade 1

"Dinner" by Jan Burkins and Kim Yaris

    I like to eat **eggs** for breakfast.

    I like to **eat** soup for lunch.

    I like to eat **meat** for dinner.

    But I like to eat ice **cream** all the time!

"Animal Noises" by Jan Burkins and Kim Yaris

The yellow cat says **meow**.

The black **cow** says moo.

The **brown** dog says woof.

The red bird says **tweet**.

What do you say?

From *Hi! Fly Guy* by Tedd Arnold (2005):

> *A boy **went** walking.*
> ***He** was looking for*
> *something to catch—*
> ***something** smart,*
> *something for*
> *The Amazing **Pet** Show.* (3–4)

Grades 2–3

From *Soupy Saturdays with the Pain & the Great One*
by Judy Blume (2007):

> On Saturdays we do errands with Dad. He's
> good at **errands**. Today, even though
> it was really warm, the Pain was **wearing**
> earmuffs. Big fluffy ones.
>
> Our first stop was the **shoe** store. The shoe
> salesman took one look at the Pain and said,
> "We have some nice snow **boots** on sale. Half
> price."
>
> "Why would I want snow **boots** in May?"
> the Pain asked.
>
> The shoe man **shrugged**. "Looks like you're
> getting **ready** for winter," he said, pointing to
> the Pain's earmuffs.
>
> "I'm getting ready for a **haircut**," the Pain
> told him.
>
> "Oh," the shoe salesman said, as if that
> made perfect **sense**.
>
> The Pain got a pair of **sandals**. So did I.
> (5–7)

Reading Wellness: Lessons in Independence and Proficiency by Jan Miller Burkins and Kim Yaris.

From *The Best Book of Spaceships* by Ian Graham (1998):

Space Suits

>In space there is no air. Anything the Sun
>**shines** on is boiling hot, and anything
>in the **shade** is freezing cold. Human
>beings cannot live in space. We need air to
>**breathe**, and we need to be at the right
>**temperature**—not too hot and not too
>cold.

>A spacecraft has to provide **astronauts**
>with air to **breathe**, and it has to keep
>them warm. When astronauts leave the
>**spacecraft**, they must wear a space
>suit, which does the same job. (20)

Reading Wellness: Lessons in Independence and Proficiency by Jan Miller Burkins and Kim Yaris.
Copyright © 2014. Stenhouse Publishers.

Grades 4–5

From *My Life in Dog Years* by Gary Paulsen (1998):

> *Fred came to me in a small cardboard box*
> *filled with wood **chips**.*
>
> *I had been in a bookstore in Bemidji,*
> *Minnesota, looking for a book on pickling fish.*
> *I love to eat **pickled** herring and had*
> *access to a large supply of small northern pike.*
>
> *It was in this uncomplicated frame of mind*
> *that I met Fred.*
>
> *I was at the curb when a small boy came up*
> *to me holding an old detergent box.*
>
> *"Hey, mister," he said with the air of a con*
> *man, "you want to buy a **puppy**?"*
>
> *"Buy?" I stopped and **peered** into the box.*
> *There was nothing but a pile of wood*
> *shavings. "What puppy?"*
>
> *"He's in there, down in the **wood**. Dig him*
> *out.*

Reading Wellness: Lessons in Independence and Proficiency by Jan Miller Burkins and Kim Yaris.

*I dug around in the **shavings** until my fingers hit the soft fur. There was a moment's hesitation, then a small growl; then a set of needle-sharp teeth **ripped** into the soft tip of my finger.*

"He bit me!"

*The boy **nodded**. "He's half Lab and half something that came into the yard one night. Dad said he'd make a great watchdog."* (90–91)

From *Immigrant Kids* by Russell Freedman (1980):

> Many **immigrants** worked from home.
> Tenement apartments became busy workshops
> where entire **families** labored seven days
> a week **sewing** clothing, making artificial
> flower rolling cigars, **shelling** nuts for
> restaurants, and performing other low-paying
> tasks. Children **worked** alongside their
> parents from the time they were old enough to
> **follow** directions. Sometimes extra workers
> were hired, and the **apartment** became
> a small factory called a "sweatshop" because
> of the **long** hours, hard work, and **low** pay.
> It was not unusual to find a dozen or more
> **people**—men, women, and children—at
> work in a stuffy tenement room. (45)

 APPENDIX C

Metaphorical Images for *Deep Breathing* Lessons

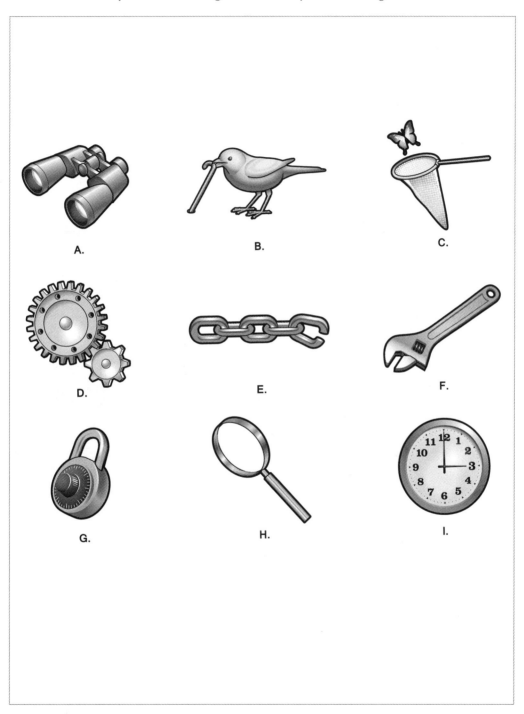

A.

B.

C.

D.

E.

F.

G.

H.

I.

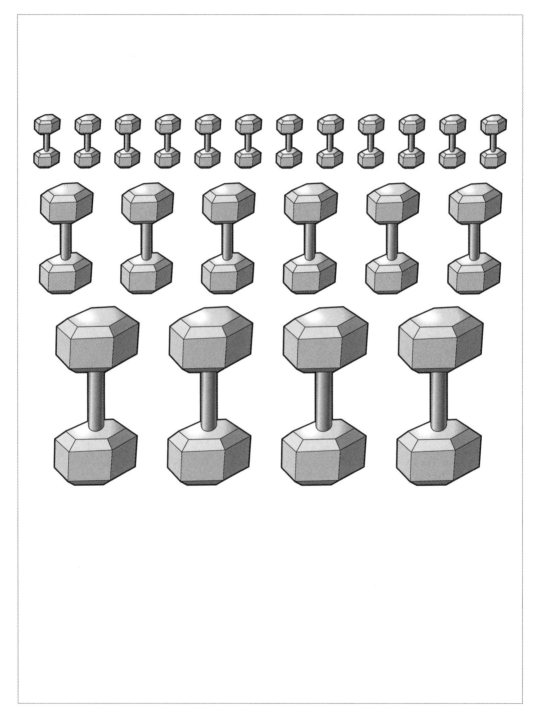

Light Effort

Best for developing fluency; least beneficial for acquiring new vocabulary.

Fastest rate; highest reading volume in a given block of time.

Relaxing; involves least effort, and all of it is productive.

There are a very few things to figure out about the print and/or the meaning, but the reader can handle all of them pretty easily with near perfect form.

Medium Effort

Develops fluency and potentially some vocabulary.

Slower rate, but the reader can still read much in a given block of time.

Mostly relaxing; involves more effort, but is still very productive.

There are some things to figure out about the print and/or the meaning, but all of them, with maybe a few exceptions, the reader can still handle independently while maintaining form.

Big Effort

Contributes less to fluency development but much more to vocabulary growth.

Slowed rate; reader reads even less in a given block of time.

Involves more focused effort, but it is still very productive.

There are many more things to figure out about the print and about the meaning, but all of them, with maybe a few exceptions, the reader can handle independently without compromising form beyond recovery.

Maximum Effort

Contributes minimally to fluency, if at all, but can contribute substantially to vocabulary growth.

Slowest rate, as reader must mostly read slowly and often reread; reader can't read for very long without fatiguing.

Manageable stress; involves extensive effort, some of which may not be productive.

There are even more things to figure out about the print and about the meaning, many of which are complex, sometimes disrupting form. Some textual challenges are beyond the reach of the reader without the support of other sources of information.

REFERENCES

Achor, Shawn. 2010. *Happiness Advantage: The Seven Principles of Positive Psychology That Fuel Success and Performance at Work.* New York: Broadway.

———. Feb. 1, 2011. "The Happy Secret to Better Work." TEDx Bloomington (Indiana). http://www.ted.com/talks/shawn_achor_the_happy_secret_to_better_work.html.

Alcott, Louisa May. 1947. *Little Women.* New York: Grosset and Dunlap.

Alverman, Donna E., Norman J. Unrau, and Robert B. Ruddell, eds. 2004. *Theoretical Models and Processes of Reading.* Newark, DE: International Reading Association.

Anderson, Greg. 1995. *The 22 Non-Negotiable Laws of Wellness: Feel, Think, and Live Better Than You Ever Thought Possible.* San Francisco: HarperCollins.

Angleberger, Tom. 2010. *The Strange Case of Origami Yoda.* New York: Amulet.

Arnold, Tedd. 2005. *Hi! Fly Guy.* New York: Scholastic.

Asim, Jabari. 2012. *Fifty Cents and a Dream: Young Booker T. Washington.* New York: Little, Brown.

Avi. 1995. *Poppy.* New York: Orchard.

Bardhan-Quallen, Sudipta. 2008. *Up Close: Jane Goodall: A Twentieth-Century Life.* New York: Penguin Group/Viking.

Barnhouse, Dorothy. 2014. *Readers Front and Center: Helping All Students Engage with Complex Texts.* Portland, ME: Stenhouse

Barnhouse, Dorothy, and Vicki Vinton. 2012. *What Readers Really Do: Teaching the Process of Meaning Making.* Portsmouth, NH. Heinemann.

Beard, Daniel Carter. 1890. *The American Boy's Handy Book: What to Do and How to Do It.* New York: Scribner.

Beck, Martha. 2001. *Finding Your Own North Star: Claiming the Life You Were Meant to Live.* New York: MJF Books.

Berg, Elizabeth. 2001. *Open House.* New York: Ballantine Books.

Berne, Jennifer. 2013. *On a Beam of Light: A Story of Albert Einstein.* San Francisco: Chronicle.

Blobaum, Cindy. 2012. *Awesome Snake Science! 40 Activities for Learning About Snakes.* Chicago: Chicago Review.

Blume, Judy. 2007. *Soupy Saturdays with the Pain & the Great One.* New York: Random House.

Borgenicht, David. 2007. *The Worst Case Scenario Survival Handbook (Junior Edition).* San Francisco: Chronicle.

Boushey, Gail, and Joan Moser. 2014. *The Daily 5, Second Edition: Fostering Literacy Independence in the Elementary Grades.* Portland, ME: Stenhouse.

Bruhn, John G., and Stewart Wolf. 2004. *The Roseto Story: An Anatomy of Health.* Norman: University of Oklahoma Press.

Bunting, Eve. 1997. *A Day's Work.* New York: Clarion.

Burkins, Jan Miller, and Melody M. Croft. 2010. *Preventing Misguided Reading: New Strategies for Guided Reading Teachers.* Newark, DE: International Reading Association.

Burroughs, Edgar Rice. 1914. *Tarzan of the Apes.* Racine, WI: Whitman.

Calkins, Lucy, Ehrenworth, Mary, and Lehman, Christopher. 2012. *Pathways to the Common Core: Accelerating Achievement.* Portsmouth, NH: Heinemann.

Cannon, Janell. 2005. *Crickwing.* New York: Harcourt.

Cisneros, Sandra. 1991. "Eleven." In *Woman Hollering Creek.* New York: Random House.

Clutton-Brock, Juliet, and Dave King. 1991. *Cat.* New York: Knopf.

Cobb, Vicki. 2008. *Your Body Battles a Broken Bone.* Minneapolis, MN: Lerner.

Common Core State Standards (CCSS). 2010. *College and Career Readiness Anchor Standards for Reading.* http://www.corestandards.org/ELA-Literacy/CCRA/R.

Cook, Deanna F. 2004. *Family Fun Super Snacks: 125 Quick Snacks That Are Fun to Make and to Eat.* New York: Disney Editions.

Covey, Stephen R. 1989. *The Seven Habits of Highly Effective People.* New York: Simon and Schuster.

———. 1994. *First Things First.* New York: Fireside.

Croza, Laura. 2010. *I Know Here.* Toronto, ON: Groundwood.

D'Agnese, Joseph. 2010. *Blockhead: The Life of Fibonacci.* New York: Henry Holt.

Dahl, Roald. 1961. *James and the Giant Peach: A Children's Story.* New York: Knopf.

———. 1982. *The BFG.* New York: Farrar, Straus and Giroux.

———. 1983. *The Witches.* New York: Farrar, Straus and Giroux.

de Saint-Exupéry, Antoine. 1943. *The Little Prince.* New York: Harcourt Brace.

Dinardo, Jeff. 2010. *Space Cat.* Egremont, MA: Red Chair.

Dunn, H. L. 1961. *High-Level Wellness.* Arlington, VA: R. W. Beatty.

Dweck, Carol S. 2006. *Mindset: The New Psychology of Success.* New York: Ballantine Books.

Edmundson, Mark. 2004. *Why Read?* New York: Bloomsbury.

El Nabli, Dina. 2008. *Henry Ford: Putting the World on Wheels.* New York: HarperCollins.

Evans, Lynette. 2008. *Snakes: Strikers and Squeezers.* New York: Scholastic.

Feynman, Richard P. 1988. *"What Do You Care What Other People Think?" Further Adventures of a Curious Character.* New York: W. W. Norton.

Fisher, Douglas, and Frey, Nancy. (2009). *Background Knowledge: The Missing Piece of the Comprehension Puzzle.* Portsmouth, NH: Heinemann.

Fontes, Justine, and Ron Fontes. 2001. *Abraham Lincoln: Lawyer, Leader, Legend.* New York: DK.

Fox, Mem. 1984. *Wilfrid Gordon McDonald Partridge.* La Jolla, CA: Kane/Miller.

———. 1997. *Time for Bed.* Orlando, FL: Harcourt Brace.

———. 1998. *Tough Boris.* Orlando, FL: Harcourt Brace.

———. 2008. *Reading Magic: Why Reading Aloud to Our Children Will Change Their Lives Forever.* Orlando, FL: Harcourt.

Frazee, Marla. 2006. *Roller Coaster.* Orlando, FL: Harcourt.

Freedman, Russell. 1980. *Immigrant Kids.* New York: Scholastic.

Fullan, Michael. 2012. *Stratosphere: Integrating Technology, Pedagogy, and Change Knowledge.* Don Mills, ON: Pearson.

Fullan, Michael, Patrical Wonch Hill, and Carmel Crévola. 2006. *Breakthrough.* Thousand Oaks, CA: Corwin.

Galloway, W. Timothy. 1997. *The Inner Game of Tennis: The Classic Guide to the Mental Side of Peak Performance.* New York: Random House.

Gladwell, Malcom. 2011. *Outliers: The Story of Success.* New York: Little, Brown.

Gleick, James. 1993. *Genius: The Life and Science of Richard Feynman.* New York: Random House/Pantheon.

Graham, Ian. 1998. *The Best Book of Spaceships.* New York: Scholastic.

Guthrie, John. April 15, 2013. "Attaining the CCSS Is Impossible—Without Engagement." *Reading Today Online.* http://www.reading.org/general/Publications/blog/BlogSinglePost/literacy-research-panel/2013/04/12/attaining-the-ccss-is-impossible-without-engagement#.UmWgUNJJNA0.

Hanh, Thich Nhat. 2011. *Planting Seeds: Practicing Mindfulness with Children.* Berkeley, CA: Parallax.

Henkes, Kevin. 2006. *Lilly's Purple Plastic Purse.* New York: HarperCollins/Greenwillow Books.

———. 2008. *Chrysanthemum.* New York: HarperCollins/Greenwillow Books.

Henson, Heather. 2008. *That Book Woman.* New York: Atheneum.

Hesse, Karen. 1999. *Come On, Rain!* New York: Scholastic.

Hindley, Joanne. 1996. *In the Company of Children.* Portland, ME: Stenhouse.

Hoffman, Mary. 1991. *Amazing Grace.* New York: Penguin/Dial Books.

Holdaway, Don. 1979. *The Foundations of Literacy*. Sydney, Australia: Scholastic.

Hooks, Bell. 1994. *Teaching to Transgress: Education as the Practice of Freedom*. New York: Routledge.

Horowitz, Alexandra. 2013. *On Looking: Eleven Walks with Expert Eyes*. New York: Simon and Schuster/Scribner.

Jeffers, Oliver. 2007. *The Incredible Book Eating Boy*. New York: Penguin/Philomel Books.

Johnson, Steven. 2010. *Where Good Ideas Come From: The Natural History of Innovation*. New York: Riverhead Books.

Johnston, Peter H. 2004. *Choice Words: How Our Language Affects Children's Learning*. Portland, ME: Stenhouse.

———. 2012. *Opening Minds: Using Language to Change Lives*. Portland, ME: Stenhouse.

Jordan, Deloris, with Roslyn M. Jordan. 2003. *Salt in His Shoes: Michael Jordan in Pursuit of a Dream*. New York: Simon and Schuster.

Joyce, William. 2012. *The Fantastic Flying Books of Mr. Morris Lessmore*. New York: Simon and Schuster/Atheneum.

Kabat-Zinn, Jon. 2005. *Wherever You Go, There You Are*. London: Piatkus.

King, Stephen. 2001. *On Writing: A Memoir of the Craft*. New York: Simon and Schuster.

Kinney, Jeff. 2007. *Diary of a Wimpy Kid*. New York: Abrams.

Krauss, Ruth. 1945. *The Carrot Seed*. New York: Harper and Brothers.

Krulik, Nancy. 2003. *I Hate Rules!* New York: Grosset and Dunlap.

Krull, Kathleen. 2000. *Wilma Unlimited: How Wilma Rudolph Became the World's Fastest Woman*. San Diego: Harcourt.

Laminack, Lester. 2010. *Snow Day!* Atlanta: Peachtree.

Lamott, Anne. 2013. *Stitches: A Handbook on Meaning, Hope and Repair*. New York: Riverhead.

Lehn, Barbara. 1999. *What Is a Scientist?* Brookfield, CT: Millbrook.

Lehman, Chris, and Kate Roberts. 2013. *Falling in Love with Close Reading: Lessons for Analyzing Texts—and Life*. Portsmouth, NH: Heinemann.

Lehrer, Jonah. 2012. *Imagine*. Boston: Houghton Mifflin Harcourt.

Lionni, Leo. 1960. *Inch by Inch*. New York: I. Obolensky.

Lipkowitz, Daniel. 2011. *The Lego Ideas Book*. Toronto, ON: Éditions Scholastic.

Little, Jean. 1986. *Hey World, Here I Am!* Toronto, ON: Kids Can.

Litwin, Eric. 2011. *Pete the Cat*. New York: Harper.

Lobel, Arnold. 1979. *Days with Frog and Toad*. New York: Harper Collins.

Lofting, Hugh. 1920. *The Story of Dr. Dolittle*. Philadelphia: Lippincott.

Logue, Mary. 2012. *Sleep Like a Tiger*. Boston: Houghton Mifflin.

Lovell, Patty. 2001. *Stand Tall, Molly Lou Melon.* New York: G. P. Putnam's Sons.

Mack, Jeff. 2012. *Good News, Bad News.* San Francisco: Chronicle.

Martin, Bill Jr. 1996. *Brown Bear, Brown Bear, What Do You See?* New York: Henry Holt.

MacDonald, Amy. 1993. *Rachel Fister's Blister.* Boston: Houghton Mifflin.

MacLachlan, Patricia. 1998. *What You Know First.* New York: HarperTrophy.

MacLeod, Elizabeth. 2004. *Marie Curie: A Brilliant Life.* Toronto, ON: Kids Can.

Maley, Alan. 2010. "The Teacher as Circus Performer." *Humanising Language Teaching.* http://www.hltmag.co.uk/aug10/sart08.htm.

Martin, Jacqueline Briggs. 2009. *Snowflake Bentley.* Boston: Houghton Mifflin Harcourt.

McBratney, Sam. 2008. *Guess How Much I Love You.* Somerville, MA: Candlewick.

McCully, Emily A. 1997. *Mirette on the High Wire.* New York: Putnam and Grosset.

McDonnell, Patrick. 2011. *Me . . . Jane.* New York: Little, Brown.

Meschenmoser, Sebastian. 2013. *Learning to Fly.* La Jolla, CA: Kane/Miller.

Miller, Debbie. 2013. *Reading with Meaning: Teaching Comprehension in the Primary Grades.* 2nd ed. Portland, ME: Stenhouse.

Muth, Jon J. 2002. *The Three Questions.* New York: Scholastic.

———. 2008. *Zen Ties.* New York: Scholastic.

Nelson, Robin. 2003. *Toys and Games Then and Now.* Minneapolis, MN: Lerner.

Newkirk, Thomas. 2011. *The Art of Slow Reading: Six Time-Honored Practices for Engagement.* Portsmouth, NH: Heinemann.

Nieto, Sonia. 2003. *What Keeps Teachers Going.* New York: Teachers College Press.

———. 2005. *Why We Teach.* New York: Teachers College Press.

Nobisso, Josephine. 2002. *In English, of Course.* Westhampton Beach, NY: Gingerbread House.

Osborne, Mary Pope. 1992. *Dinosaurs Before Dark.* New York: Random House.

———. 1998. *Lions at Lunchtime.* New York: Random House.

Osborne, Will, and Mary Pope Osborne. 2000. *Dinosaurs.* New York: Random House.

Otoshi, Kathryn. 2008. *One.* San Rafael, CA: KO Kids Books.

Park, Barbara. 1993. *Junie B. Jones and a Little Monkey Business.* New York: Random House.

Paulsen, Gary. 1987. *Hatchet.* New York: Simon and Schuster/Aladdin.

———. 1998. *My Life in Dog Years.* New York: Random House.

Pausch, Randy. 2008. *The Last Lecture.* New York: Hyperion.

Pearson, P. David, and Margaret C. Gallagher. 1983. "The Instruction of Reading Comprehension." *Contemporary Educational Psychology* 8 (3): 317–344.

Penn, Audrey. 1993. *The Kissing Hand.* Washington, D.C.: Child Welfare League of America.

Perez, Amada Irma. 2009. *My Diary from Here to There.* San Francisco: Children's Book Press.

Pigdon, Keith. 2003. "A Storm Is Coming." Explorations series. Temecula, CA: Okapi.

Pink, Daniel. 2006. *A Whole New Mind: Why Right-Brainers Will Rule the Future.* New York: Penguin Group.

Pinkwater, Daniel Manus. 1993. *The Big Orange Splot.* New York: Scholastic.

Pyers, Greg. 2000. *Animal Feet.* Melbourne, Australia: Pearson.

Quindlen, Anna. 1998. *How Reading Changed My Life.* New York: Random House.

Rathman, Peggy. 1996. *Goodnight, Gorilla!* New York: Puffin Books.

Rawls, Wilson. 1961. *Where the Red Fern Grows.* New York: Bantam Doubleday Dell.

Reynolds, Peter H. 2004. *Ish.* Cambridge, MA: Candlewick.

Riordan, Rick. 2008. *39 Clues.* New York: Scholastic.

———. 2010. *The Lost Hero.* New York: Hyperion.

Robinson, Fiona. 2011. *What Animals Really Like.* New York: Abrams Books.

Rosenblatt, Louise M. 2004. "The Transaction Theory of Reading and Writing." In *Theoretical Models and Processes of Reading.* 5th ed., ed. Robert B. Ruddell and Norman J. Unrau. Newark, DE: International Reading Association.

Rowling, J. K. 1999. *Harry Potter and the Sorcerer's Stone.* New York: Scholastic.

Rylant, Cynthia. 1997. *Silver Packages: An Appalachian Christmas Story.* New York: Orchard Books.

———. 2005. *Henry and Mudge and the Tumbling Trip.* New York: Simon and Schuster.

Rubin, Gretchen. 2009. *The Happiness Project: Why I Spent a Year Trying to Sing in the Morning, Clean My Closets, Fight Right, Read Aristotle, and Generally Have More Fun.* New York: HarperCollins.

Sachar, Louis. 2000. *Holes.* New York: Random House/Yearling.

Sayre, April Pulley. 2008. *Trout Are Made of Trees.* Watertown, MA: Charlesbridge.

Scieszka, Jon. 1992. *The Stinky Cheese Man and Other Fairly Stupid Tales.* New York: Penguin Books/Viking.

Sendak, Maurice. 1963. *Where the Wild Things Are.* New York: HarperCollins.

Seuss, Dr. 1960. *Green Eggs and Ham.* New York: Random House.

Shanahan, Timothy, Douglas Fisher, and Nancy Frey. 2012. "The Challenge of Challenging Text." *Educational Leadership* (69) 6: 58–62.

Silverstein, Shel. 1964. *The Giving Tree.* New York: HarperCollins.

Spinelli, Eileen. 1996. *Somebody Loves You, Mr. Hatch.* New York: Simon and Schuster.

———. 2004. *Sophie's Masterpiece.* New York: Simon and Schuster.

———. 2007. *Someday.* New York: Penguin/Dial.

Stein, David Ezra. 2012. *Because Amelia Smiled.* Somerville, MA: Candlewick.

Sweet, Melissa. 2011. *Balloons Over Broadway: The True Story of the Puppeteer of Macy's Parade.* New York: Houghton Mifflin Harcourt.

Taveres, Matt. 2000. *Zachary's Ball.* Somerville, MA: Candlewick.

Thomas, Peggy. 2011. *For the Birds: The Life of Roger Tory Peterson.* Honesdale, PA: Boyds Mill/Calkins Creek.

Tovani, Cris. 2004. *Do I Really Have to Teach Reading? Content Comprehension, Grades 6–12.* Portland, ME: Stenhouse.

Tullet, Hervé. 2011. *Press Here.* San Francisco: Chronicle Books.

Twain, Mark. 1885. *Adventures of Huckleberry Finn.* New York: Charles L. Webster.

———. 1989. *Following the Equator: A Journey Around the World.* Mineola, NY: Dover.

United Nations Office of the High Commissioner for Human Rights. Universal Declaration of Human Rights, adopted and proclaimed by General Assembly Resolution 217 A (III) of 10 December 1948, from http://www.un.org/en/documents/udhr/.

Van Allsburg, Chris. 1991. *The Wretched Stone.* New York: Houghton Mifflin.

———. 1993. *The Sweetest Fig.* Boston: Houghton Mifflin.

Viorst, Judith. 1987. *Alexander and the Terrible, Horrible, No Good, Very Bad Day*. New York: Atheneum.

———. 1987. *The Tenth Good Thing About Barney.* New York: Simon and Schuster/Aladdin.

———. 1993. *Earrings!* New York: Simon and Schuster.

Waldman, Neil. 2011. *A Land of Big Dreamers: Voices of Courage in America.* Minneapolis, MN: Lerner Publishing Group/Millbrook Press.

Wallace, Karen. 1998. *Tale of a Tadpole.* New York: DK.

White, Elwyn Brooks. 1952. *Charlotte's Web.* New York: Harper.

Willems, Mo. 2005. *Leonardo, The Terrible Monster.* New York: Hyperion.

———. 2010. *Are You Ready to Play Outside?* New York: Disney/Hyperion.

———. 2010. *Can I Play Too?* New York: Disney/Hyperion.

———. 2010. *City Dog, Country Frog.* New York: Disney/Hyperion.

———. 2012. *Let's Go for a Drive!* New York: Hyperion.

Williams, Vera B. 1982. *A Chair for My Mother.* New York: HarperCollins.

Wilson, Gaye. 2012. "An Extraordinary Expedition." *Cobblestone* 33 (7): 26.

Woods, Andrew. 1992. *Young Orville and Wilbur Wright: First to Fly.* Mahwah, NJ: Troll Associates.

Yaris, Kim. 2013. Personal correspondence. October 12.

Yashima, Taro. 1976. *Crow Boy.* New York: Penguin/Viking.

INDEX